Rick Gallop's
EXPRESS
Gi DIET
FOR *BUSY* PEOPLE

D0867745

50 SPEEDY RECIPES

From the author of the bestselling green-light **Gi** DIET series

Rick Gallop's

EXPRESS

Gi DIET

FOR *BUSY* PEOPLE

First published in Great Britain in 2007 by
Virgin Books Ltd
Thames Wharf Studios
Rainville Road
London
W6 9HA

A catalogue record for this book is available from the British
Library.

ISBN (10) 0 7535 1178 9
      (13) 978 0 7535 1178 7

The paper used in this book is a natural, recyclable product
made from wood grown in sustainable forests. The
manufacturing process conforms to the regulations of the
country of origin.

Designed and typeset by Virgin Books Ltd

Printed and bound in Italy

CONTENTS

INTRODUCTION

Since my first book, *The Gi Diet*, was launched some four years ago, it has sold over two million copies worldwide. It's easy to explain the book's success.

It works: Hundreds of thousands of people have lost weight permanently and painlessly without going hungry or feeling deprived.

It's simple to follow: There's no counting calories or points. No weighing and measuring foods. All foods are traffic-light colour-coded so all you have to do is follow the green light.

It's healthy and nutritious: Unlike many diets, the Gi Diet is healthy and balanced. It will guide you for the rest of your life.

Unbelievably, I've received a flood of over 25,000 e-mails from readers. These have given me a great insight into the challenges my readers face when trying to improve their lifestyle and diet. Many of you requested more recipes, more information on shopping and eating out, and more tips on dealing with reluctant spouses and finicky children. This prompted me to write new recipe books – *Living the Gi Diet* and *The Green Light Cookbook* – as well as *The Gi Diet Shopping and Eating Out Pocket Guide* and *The Family Gi Diet*.

More recently, your e-mails have focused on the time pressures you face on a daily basis. How do you manage the Gi

Diet on a hectic schedule? With demanding jobs, busy family lives and the fact that there are simply not enough hours in the day, many of you admit to letting matters of health and weight take a back seat.

Help is at hand! The Express Gi Diet has been created precisely with you busy people in mind. It offers simple, practical advice on shopping and stocking the pantry with the right green light essentials, suggestions for on-the-run and sit-down breakfasts, packed lunches and eating out in fast-food restaurants, plus dozens of delicious dinner recipes and tasty snacks to keep you going. Everything is quick and easy to prepare.

'The Express Gi Diet means you'll never be too busy to lose weight!'

I've also included some advice on exercise and how to incorporate it into your day.

My wife, Dr Ruth Gallop, who co-authored *The Family Gi Diet*, has been my partner for 35 years. During that time, she has played an executive role in all matters of nutrition and health in our household of three boys. For this book, she has written most of the sections on food preparation, along with the recipes, in conjunction with her close friend and food expert Natalie Stein. We've also had the advice and counsel of the brilliant young cook Laura Buckley.

Now you no longer have the excuse of being too busy to manage your weight and look after your health. *The Express*

Gi Diet builds on the hugely successful Gi Diet, which has changed the lives of literally tens of thousands of readers, by adapting it to meet the needs of your busy life.

If you are interested in receiving the **free quarterly Gi Diet Newsletter**, simply go to www.gidiet.com and sign up. The website also features readers' comments, medical and media reviews, as well as reports on new developments in health and nutrition.

You can also contact me through this website – I love to hear about your experiences, comments and suggestions.

ENJOY!

CHAPTER 1: THE GI DIET IN A NUTSHELL

WHAT DOES 'GI' ACTUALLY MEAN?

Gi stands for Glycaemic Index, a medical term used to measure the speed at which carbohydrates break down in the digestive system to form glucose (sugar). Glucose is the body's source of energy; it is the fuel that feeds your brain, muscles and other organs. Sugar is set at 100 and all foods are indexed against that number. Therefore, foods that are digested quickly have a high Gi and foods that are digested slowly have a low Gi.

'Low Gi foods are digested slowly, high Gi foods are digested quickly'

Here are some popular examples, showing high Gi foods in the left column and low Gi foods in the right.

EXAMPLES OF Gi RATINGS

High Gi		Low Gi*	
Foods	Rating	Foods	Rating
Sugar	100	Orange	44
Baguette	95	All Bran	43
Cornflakes	84	Oatmeal	42
Rice cakes	82	Spaghetti	41
Doughnut	76	Apples	38
Bagel	72	Beans	31
Cereal bar	72	Grapefruit	25
Biscuits (plain)	69	Yoghurt	14

* Any food rating less than 55 in the Gi is considered low

SUGAR RUSH

So what's all this got to do with losing weight? Lots, actually! When you eat high Gi foods such as cornflakes, your body rapidly converts the food into glucose, which dissolves in your bloodstream, spiking your blood-sugar level and giving you that familiar sugar rush, or high. On the other hand, a low Gi food, such as porridge, will break down more slowly and deliver glucose into the bloodstream at a slower, steadier (and therefore preferable) rate.

The following chart demonstrates the different impact of high and low Gi foods on your blood-sugar levels.

Gi IMPACT ON SUGAR LEVELS

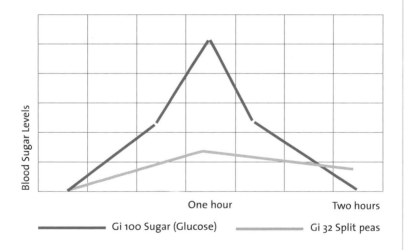

Blood Sugar Levels

One hour   Two hours

━━━━━ Gi 100 Sugar (Glucose)   ━━━━━ Gi 32 Split peas

This sugar rush is short-lived because of a critical enzyme called insulin. Insulin's role is to take sugar from the bloodstream and store it for immediate use in the muscles, or as fat around the waist, hips and thighs. The higher the sugar spike, the more insulin is released and the quicker the sugar is drained from your bloodstream, leaving you with a sugar low.

You know what happens then, don't you? You start looking for your next sugar fix. That's why after your high Gi breakfast of sugary, cold cereal, you inevitably find yourself picking up a cappuccino and croissant on your way to work. It's clear – a diet made up of high Gi foods makes you feel hungry more often. The result? You eat more.

'Low Gi foods leave you feeling fuller for longer, so you won't go craving that sugar fix'

At the other end of the spectrum, low Gi foods deliver a steady stream of glucose because they break down more slowly, and don't trigger a sugar spike or a flood of insulin. As a result, you feel fuller for longer and eat less without going hungry. This is the key to any successful diet, and precisely the reason why the Gi Diet is so popular.

Up to now, we have been focusing on carbs (carbohydrates), which account for over half of our energy needs. But we also have two other critical food groups to consider, namely proteins and fats.

THE LOWDOWN ON PROTEIN

Proteins are essential for our health. Half of our dry body weight is made up of protein, including muscles, organs, skin and hair. Protein is needed to build and repair body tissue. It is also very effective at satisfying hunger as it acts as a brake on the digestive system. Much like low Gi carbohydrates, protein helps you feel fuller for longer. Unfortunately, much of our protein comes from animal sources, which are usually high in saturated or 'bad' fat. Lean protein found in lean meats, fish, poultry and soya are your best green light choices.

THE LOWDOWN ON FAT

Fat is also essential for our health and body functions. However, many fats are positively dangerous and can actually increase the risk of heart disease, stroke and cancer. These are called saturated fats and they are normally solid at room temperature: things like cheese, butter and fatty meats. Even worse are trans fats or hydrogenated fats, which have been processed to make them thicken. These are found in packets of biscuits, crisps and other snacks. Your best choices are polyunsaturated fats, such as most vegetable oils; monosaturated fats, such as olive, rapeseed, peanut, safflower oils and most nuts, which are particularly good for you; and omega-3, an oil found in deep-sea fish such as salmon, as well as in flaxseed, which is great for the heart. However, as fats have over twice the amount of calories per gram as carbs and proteins, it's a good idea to keep quantities down.

SUMMARY

The ideal combination of foods is low Gi carbohydrates, lean protein, and monosaturated/polyunsaturated fats.

TRAFFIC LIGHTS

So that you don't have to bother about calculating Gi ratings, calorie counts and saturated-fat levels, we have done all the maths for you. For simplification purposes, results have been colour-coded into three traffic-light colours.

RED LIGHT FOODS

High Gi and high calorie foods. Do not eat these if you want to lose weight.

YELLOW LIGHT FOODS

Mid-range Gi foods. Eat these when you have reached your target weight.

GREEN LIGHT FOODS

These foods are low Gi, low in calories and low in saturated (bad) fat. With a few exceptions (see below), you can eat as much of these foods as you like. However, as with all things, everything in moderation – don't go completely overboard!

RECOMMENDED GREEN LIGHT SERVINGS

Green light breads (these have at least 2½–3g of fibre per slice)	1 slice
Green light cereals	120g (4oz)
Green light nuts	8–10g (small handful)
Margarine (non-hydrogenated, light)	2tsp
Meat, fish, poultry	120g (4oz) (the size of a pack of cards)
Olive/vegetable oil	1tsp
Olives	4–5
Pasta	40g (1½oz) uncooked
Potatoes (new, boiled)	2–3
Rice (basmati, brown, long-grain)	50g (1¾oz) uncooked
Phase II	
Chocolate (at least 70% cocoa)	2 squares
Red wine	1 glass (125ml/5fl oz)

MEALS

Make sure you eat three main meals per day, plus three snacks between meals – mid-morning, mid-afternoon and before bed. The important thing is to keep your blood-sugar levels constant and avoid the sugar highs and lows that are the usual reasons why people overeat. Keeping your tummy busy and your blood-sugar levels constant is fundamental to the success of the Gi Diet.

'Remember: three meals and three snacks a day, and you won't go wrong'

PORTIONS

Each meal and snack should contain a combination of green light carbohydrates, protein and fats. Visualise your dinner plate divided into four quarters. Then fill two quarters with vegetables, one quarter with meat/fish/poultry/tofu and the remaining quarter with rice/pasta/potatoes.

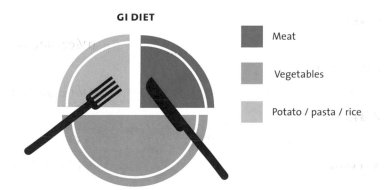

GI DIET

- Meat
- Vegetables
- Potato / pasta / rice

TIMING

There are two phases to the Gi Diet.

PHASE ONE – THE WEIGHT LOSS PHASE

During this phase you should eat green light foods only. You should lose an average of ½ kg (1lb) per week. If you have a significant amount of weight to lose, then you should lose 1kg (2lb) or more per week.

PHASE TWO – THE MAINTENANCE PHASE

This begins once you've reached your target weight. You can now eat yellow light foods. This is how you will eat for the rest of your life.

SUMMARY

- Low Gi foods are digested more slowly, so you feel satisfied for longer
- Green light foods are key to losing weight as they are low Gi, low in calories and low in saturated fats
- During phase one, eat only green light foods
- Eat three balanced meals and three snacks per day

CHAPTER 2: GETTING STARTED

There are three simple steps to getting started on the Express Gi Diet.

● **Set your weight loss target**

● Clear out your pantry/fridge

● Go supermarket green light shopping

WEIGHT LOSS TARGET: HOW MUCH WEIGHT DO YOU WANT TO LOSE?

The amount of weight you want to lose is a very personal decision. However, follow these guidelines and you won't go far wrong.

BODY MASS INDEX (BMI)

BMI is the only internationally accepted measurement for assessing how much body fat you are carrying relative to your height. Use the BMI table on pages 17-18 to find your height in the horizontal line across the top. Go down the vertical line on the left to find your current weight. You will find your BMI at the point where the two columns meet.

BMI TABLE

WEIGHT				HEIGHT																			
BRITISH		US		FT INS	4'6"	4'8"	4'10"	5'0"	5'2"	5'3"	5'4"	5'5"	5'6"	5'7"	5'8"	5'9"	5'10"	5'11"	6'0"	6'2"	6'4"	6'6"	6'8"
STONES	LBS	POUNDS	KILOS	CM	137	142	147	152	157	160	163	165	168	170	173	175	178	180	183	188	193	198	203
6	7	91	41		22.0	20.4	19.0	17.8	16.6	16.1	15.6	15.1	14.7	14.3	13.8	13.4	13.1	12.7	12.3	11.7	11.1	10.5	10.0
6	10	94	43		22.7	21.1	19.6	18.4	17.2	16.7	16.1	15.6	15.2	14.7	14.3	13.9	13.5	13.1	12.7	12.1	11.4	10.9	10.3
7	0	98	44		23.7	22.0	20.5	19.1	17.9	17.4	16.8	16.3	15.8	15.3	14.9	14.5	14.1	13.7	13.3	12.6	11.9	11.3	10.8
7	3	101	46		24.4	22.6	21.1	19.7	18.5	17.9	17.3	16.8	16.3	15.8	15.4	14.9	14.5	14.1	13.7	13.0	12.3	11.7	11.1
7	7	105	48		25.4	23.5	21.9	20.5	19.2	18.6	18.0	17.5	16.9	16.4	16.0	15.5	15.1	14.6	14.2	13.5	12.8	12.1	11.5
7	10	108	49		26.1	24.2	22.6	21.1	19.8	19.1	18.5	18.0	17.4	16.9	16.4	15.9	15.5	15.1	14.6	13.9	13.1	12.5	11.9
8	0	112	51		27.1	25.1	23.4	21.9	20.5	19.8	19.2	18.6	18.1	17.5	17.0	16.5	16.1	15.6	15.2	14.4	13.6	12.9	12.3
8	3	115	52		27.8	25.8	24.0	22.5	21.0	20.4	19.7	19.1	18.6	18.1	17.5	17.0	16.5	16.0	15.6	14.8	14.0	13.3	12.6
8	7	119	54		28.8	26.7	24.9	23.2	21.8	21.1	20.4	19.8	19.2	18.6	18.1	17.6	17.1	16.6	16.1	15.3	14.5	13.8	13.1
8	10	122	55		29.5	27.4	25.5	23.8	22.3	21.6	20.9	20.3	19.7	19.1	18.5	18.0	17.5	17.0	16.5	15.7	14.9	14.1	13.4
9	3	129	59		31.2	28.9	27.0	25.2	23.6	22.9	22.1	21.5	20.8	20.2	19.6	19.0	18.5	18.0	17.5	16.6	15.7	14.9	14.2
9	7	133	60		32.1	29.8	27.8	26.0	24.3	23.6	22.8	22.1	21.5	20.8	20.2	19.6	19.1	18.5	18.0	17.1	16.2	15.4	14.6
9	10	136	62		32.9	30.5	28.4	26.6	24.9	24.1	23.3	22.6	21.9	21.3	20.7	20.1	19.6	19.0	18.4	17.5	16.6	15.7	14.9
10	0	140	64		33.8	31.4	29.3	27.3	25.6	24.8	24.0	23.3	22.6	21.9	21.3	20.7	20.1	19.5	19.0	18.0	17.0	16.2	15.4
10	3	143	65		34.5	32.1	29.9	27.9	26.0	25.3	24.5	23.8	23.1	22.4	21.7	21.1	20.5	19.9	19.5	18.4	17.4	16.5	15.7
10	7	147	67		35.5	33.0	30.7	28.7	26.6	26.0	25.2	24.5	23.7	23.0	22.4	21.7	21.1	20.5	19.9	18.9	17.9	17.0	16.1
10	10	150	68		36.3	33.6	31.3	29.3	27.4	26.6	25.7	25.0	24.2	23.5	22.8	22.2	21.5	20.9	20.3	19.3	18.3	17.3	16.5
11	0	154	70		37.2	34.5	32.2	30.1	28.2	27.3	26.4	25.6	24.9	24.1	23.4	22.7	22.1	21.5	20.9	19.8	18.7	17.8	16.9
11	3	157	71		37.9	35.2	32.8	30.3	28.7	27.8	26.9	26.1	25.3	24.6	23.9	23.2	22.5	21.9	21.3	20.2	19.1	18.1	17.2
11	7	161	73		38.9	36.1	33.6	31.4	29.4	28.5	27.6	26.8	26.0	25.2	24.5	23.8	23.1	22.5	21.8	20.7	19.6	18.6	17.7
11	10	164	74		39.6	36.8	34.3	32.0	30.0	29.1	28.2	27.3	26.5	25.7	24.9	24.2	23.5	22.9	22.2	21.1	20.0	19.0	18.0
12	0	168	76		40.6	37.7	35.1	32.8	30.7	29.8	28.8	28.0	27.1	26.3	25.5	24.8	24.1	23.4	22.8	21.6	20.4	19.4	18.5
12	3	171	78		41.3	38.3	35.7	33.4	31.3	30.3	29.4	28.5	27.6	26.8	26.0	25.3	24.5	23.8	23.2	22.0	20.8	19.8	18.8
12	7	175	79		42.3	39.2	36.6	34.2	32.0	31.0	30.0	29.1	28.2	27.4	26.6	25.8	25.1	24.4	23.7	22.5	21.3	20.2	19.2

12	81	10	178	43.0	39.9	37.2	34.8	32.6	31.5	30.6	29.6	28.7	27.9	27.1	26.3	25.5	24.8	24.1	22.9	21.7	20.6	19.6
13	83	0	182	44.0	40.8	38.0	35.5	33.3	32.2	31.2	30.3	29.4	28.5	27.7	26.9	26.1	25.4	24.7	23.4	22.2	21.0	20.0
13	84	3	185	44.7	41.5	38.7	36.1	33.8	32.8	31.8	30.8	29.9	29.0	28.1	27.3	26.5	25.8	25.1	23.8	22.5	21.4	20.3
13	86	7	189	45.7	42.4	39.5	36.9	34.6	33.5	32.4	31.5	30.5	29.6	28.7	27.9	27.1	26.4	25.6	24.3	23.0	21.8	20.8
13	87	10	192	46.4	43.0	40.1	37.5	35.1	34.0	33.0	31.9	31.0	30.1	29.2	28.4	27.5	26.8	26.0	24.7	23.4	22.2	21.1
14	89	0	196	47.4	43.9	41.0	38.3	35.8	34.7	33.6	32.6	31.6	30.7	29.8	28.9	28.1	27.3	26.6	25.2	23.9	22.6	21.5
14	90	3	199	48.1	44.6	41.6	38.9	36.4	35.3	34.2	33.1	32.1	31.2	30.3	29.4	28.6	27.8	27.0	25.5	24.2	23.0	21.9
14	92	7	203	49.1	45.5	42.4	39.6	37.1	36.0	34.8	33.8	32.8	31.8	30.9	30.0	29.1	28.3	27.5	26.1	24.7	23.5	22.3
14	93	10	206	49.8	46.2	43.1	40.2	37.7	36.5	35.4	34.3	33.3	32.3	31.3	30.4	29.6	28.7	27.9	26.4	25.1	23.8	22.6
15	95	0	210	50.8	47.1	43.9	41.0	38.4	37.2	36.0	34.9	33.9	32.9	31.9	31.0	30.1	29.3	28.5	27.0	25.6	24.3	23.1
15	97	3	213	51.5	47.8	44.5	41.6	39.0	37.7	36.6	35.4	34.4	33.4	32.4	31.5	30.6	29.7	28.9	27.3	25.9	24.6	23.4
15	98	7	217	52.4	48.6	45.4	42.4	39.7	38.4	37.2	36.1	35.0	34.0	33.0	32.0	31.1	30.3	29.4	27.9	26.4	25.1	23.8
15	100	10	220	53.2	49.3	46.0	43.0	40.2	39.0	37.8	36.6	35.5	34.5	33.5	32.5	31.6	30.7	29.8	28.2	26.8	25.4	24.2
16	102	0	224	54.1	50.2	46.8	43.7	41.0	39.7	38.4	37.3	36.2	35.1	34.3	33.1	32.1	31.2	30.4	28.8	27.3	25.9	24.6
16	103	3	227	54.9	50.9	47.4	44.3	41.5	40.2	39.0	37.8	36.5	35.6	34.5	33.5	32.5	31.7	30.8	29.1	27.6	26.2	24.9
16	105	7	231	55.8	51.8	48.3	45.1	42.3	40.9	39.7	38.4	37.3	36.2	35.3	34.1	33.1	32.2	31.3	29.7	28.1	26.7	25.4
16	106	10	234	56.6	52.5	48.9	45.7	42.8	41.5	40.2	38.9	37.8	36.6	35.6	34.6	33.6	32.6	31.7	30.0	28.5	27.0	25.7
17	108	0	238	57.5	53.4	49.7	46.5	43.5	42.2	40.9	39.5	38.4	37.3	36.2	35.1	34.1	33.2	32.3	30.6	29.0	27.5	26.1
17	111	7	245	59.0	54.9	51.2	47.8	44.8	43.3	42.0	40.7	39.5	38.3	37.3	36.1	35.1	34.1	33.2	31.4	29.8	28.3	26.9
18	114	0	252	60.7	56.4	52.6	49.3	46.0	44.6	43.2	41.9	40.6	39.4	38.3	37.2	36.1	35.1	34.1	32.3	30.5	29.1	27.6
18	117	7	259	62.4	58.0	54.1	50.5	47.3	45.8	44.4	43.0	41.8	40.5	39.3	38.2	37.1	36.1	35.1	33.2	31.5	29.9	28.4
19	120	0	266	64.1	59.6	55.5	51.9	48.6	47.1	45.6	44.2	42.9	41.6	40.4	39.2	38.1	37.0	36.0	34.1	32.3	30.7	29.2

Now check your results against the following BMI standards.

BMI RATING	INDICATIONS
19–24	Healthy
25–29	Overweight
30–39	Obese
40 plus	Morbidly obese

Please note, if you have a particularly large or small frame or you are heavily muscled, these ratings may not be wholly accurate.

WAIST MEASUREMENT: WHERE, EXACTLY, IS YOUR PROBLEM AREA?

Recent research has shown that fat stored around the belly, rather than on other parts of the body, represents the greatest health risk. If you are carrying most of your surplus weight around your middle (described as being 'apple-shaped'), you are more at risk than if you carry it around your hips (described as being 'pear-shaped'). Check out your waistline, measured at the navel, against the following guidelines, to see if your excess weight is putting your health at risk.

Healthy	Some Health Risk	Serious Health Risk
Women		
under 90cm (35in.)	90–94cm (35–37in.)	over 94cm (37in.)
Men		
under 94cm (37in.)	94–100cm (37–40in.)	over 100cm (40in.)

WAIST-TO-HIP RATIO

Another way of looking at the 'apple' versus 'pear' shape is by working out your waist-to-hip ratio. This is calculated by dividing your waist measurement by your hip measurement (i.e. the widest part of your bottom).

HEALTHY RATIOS

Women with a healthy ratio are those who have a waist to hip ratio of 0.80 or under, i.e. their waist measures 80 per cent (or less) of their hips.

Men with a healthy ratio are those who have a waist to hip ratio of 0.95 or under, i.e. their waist measures 95% (or less) of their hips.

These three measurements (BMI, waist, and waist-to-hip ratio) will help you set your weight loss targets.

TIMELINES: HOW LONG WILL IT TAKE ME TO REACH MY TARGET WEIGHT?

As we've already mentioned, in general terms you should be looking at losing an average of ½ kg (1lb) per week. If you are considerably overweight, this could increase to an average of 1kg (2lb) per week or more.

Remember, weight loss rarely occurs in a straight line but rather in a series of plateaus or steps. Don't panic if nothing happens for a week or two – wait for your body to adjust and the weight will eventually fall off.

Weigh yourself once a week (and once a week only), on the same day of the week and at the same time, preferably just before breakfast. A meal or bowel movement can make quite a difference!

'Don't worry if your weight loss isn't immediate – your body needs time to adjust to the new way of eating'

CLEAR OUT YOUR PANTRY/FRIDGE

Before you go shopping for your green light foods, it's vital you clear the decks and toss out those red light foods that you won't be needing in your new life. This will remove temptation and send a clear signal to your partner or family that things are about to change for the better. If you're uncomfortable wasting food, just offer your unwanted red light items to charity or to your skinny neighbours.

SHOPPING

Never go shopping on an empty stomach or you could find yourself lunging for those tempting red light foods at the checkout.

The next chapter, which tells you all you need to know about green light shopping, has been organised by department or aisle – Fruit and Vegetable Aisle, Deli Counter, Bakery, etc. – so you can quickly identify where to find your favourite green light foods.

Because it would be impossible to list every brand in today's huge supermarkets, we have elected to list food by category. For example, we list 'Porridge Oats' and not 'Scott's Porridge Oats'. In a few instances, where there is clearly a preferable option, we make an exception and list the food by its brand name.

In the current competitive marketplace, most brands in any given category are fairly similar, so your choice will usually be made on quality and taste. In a few cases, where there may be some variations in content between brands – bread is a good example of this – it is well worth checking out the nutritional labels. Here is a typical label.

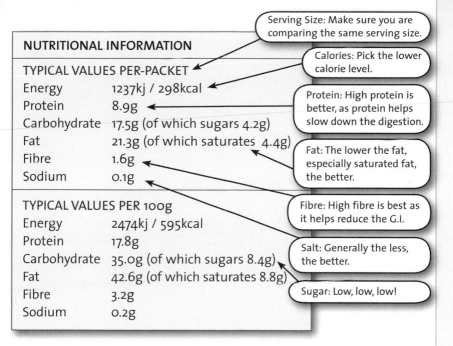

NUTRITIONAL INFORMATION

TYPICAL VALUES PER-PACKET

Energy	1237kj / 298kcal
Protein	8.9g
Carbohydrate	17.5g (of which sugars 4.2g)
Fat	21.3g (of which saturates 4.4g)
Fibre	1.6g
Sodium	0.1g

TYPICAL VALUES PER 100g

Energy	2474kj / 595kcal
Protein	17.8g
Carbohydrate	35.0g (of which sugars 8.4g)
Fat	42.6g (of which saturates 8.8g)
Fibre	3.2g
Sodium	0.2g

Serving Size: Make sure you are comparing the same serving size.

Calories: Pick the lower calorie level.

Protein: High protein is better, as protein helps slow down the digestion.

Fat: The lower the fat, especially saturated fat, the better.

Fibre: High fibre is best as it helps reduce the G.I.

Salt: Generally the less, the better.

Sugar: Low, low, low!

A very useful little table has been published by the Food Standards Authority that defines whether products have a little or a lot of four key components.

	A lot per 100g	A little per 100g
Fat	20g	3g
Saturates	5g	1g
Sugars	10g	2g
Salt	1.25g	0.25g

SUMMARY

1. Set weight/waist targets
2. Clear the decks – pantry/fridge/freezer
3. Go green light shopping

CHAPTER 3: GREEN LIGHT SHOPPING

BASIC GREEN LIGHT PANTRY

This consists of all the foods you will need for the basic meals and recipes in this book.

In each supermarket department, we list in **bold** those green light foods that are basic to the green light pantry and are commonly used in the recipes and meal suggestions in this book. This will help speed up your shopping. Other green light foods are used more occasionally – choosing them is very much a matter of your personal taste.

We have laid out the following section along the lines of the typical supermarket and have listed your best green light choices in each aisle, department or counter.

Writing a list will save you time and ensure a key food isn't forgotten. Shopping the green light way will soon become second nature and a shopping list will probably become unnecessary.

A note on supermarket brands. Several of the supermarkets have made a real effort to improve the nutritional content of their own house brands and are introducing new healthier choices. Tesco (Healthy Living), Sainsbury's (Be Good to Yourself), and Marks and Spencer (Count on Us) for instance, all have a broad range of products that generally contain less sugar, saturated fats and salt. This does not necessarily make them green light, but when in doubt about the best brand of choice in a given green light category, 'healthy' brands are usually a best buy from a nutritional and price standpoint.

FRUIT AND VEGETABLE AISLE

Vegetables

These are the cornerstone of the Gi Diet. They are low Gi but high in fibre, and contain the nutrients, vitamins and minerals that form the basis of a healthy and nutritious diet. Certain root vegetables are the exception to the rule.

As all cooking raises the Gi and reduces nutritional content, always slightly undercook food, with some firmness to the bite or *al dente*. Microwaving in a little water is the recommended way to cook from both a speed and nutrition point of view. For more on food preparation see 'Cooking Basics', page 49.

Potatoes, along with rice, are the only principal foods that have different Gi ratings dependent on what type you use, and how you cook them. Large baked potatoes are high Gi and therefore red light, as the baking process breaks down the fibre in them to make them more quickly digested. Small, preferably new, boiled potatoes have a far lower Gi. Don't mash them, as this also makes them digest more quickly. Remember, the key to the Gi Diet is slowing down the digestive process. By the way, remember that frozen vegetables and fruits have the same Gi rating and nutritional value as fresh.

Alfalfa sprouts
Asparagus
Aubergines
Beans (green/runner)
Bok choy
Broccoli
Brussels sprouts
Cabbage (all varieties)
Carrots
Cauliflower

Celeriac
Celery
Courgettes
Cucumbers
Edamame (soy beans)
Endive
Fresh herbs
Garlic
Horseradish
Kale
Leeks
Lettuce (all varieties)
Mangetout
Mushrooms (all varieties)
Mustard greens
New potatoes
Okra
Onions
Peas
Peppers (sweet or hot)
Radicchio
Radishes
Rocket
Root ginger
Shallots
Spring onions
Sugar-snap peas
Sun-dried tomatoes
Swiss chard
Tomatoes
Watercress

For a complete list of red, yellow and green light vegetables, see appendix 1 page 132.

Fruits

Virtually all fresh/frozen fruits are low Gi and green light. There are a few that are low in fibre and high in sugar such as melons (including watermelons), which are high Gi and therefore red light.

Fruits are an excellent source of fibre, vitamins and minerals, all of which are essential for good health.

Apples
Avocado
Blackberries
Cherries
Clementines
Cranberries
Grapefruit
Grapes
Guavas
Lemons
Mandarin oranges
Nectarines
Oranges
Peaches
Pears
Plums
Raspberries
Rhubarb
Strawberries
Tangerines

For a complete list of red, yellow and green light fruits see appendix 1 page 132.

THE DELI COUNTER

Most processed meats are high in saturated (bad) fat, salt
and nitrates and are therefore red light. Cheeses are generally
loaded with saturated fat, though may be sprinkled on salads,
omelettes and pasta for a little extra flavour. Lean processed
meats and low-fat cheese are your best green light options.

Processed meat
Chicken breast
Lean ham
Turkey breast

Cheese
Laughing Cow light
Boursin light
Fat-free cheese

Other
Olives
Hummus

For a complete list of red, yellow and green light deli
counter products see appendix 1 page 132.

BAKERY

A word of warning about bakery, as this can be a minefield of
misinformation. Most baked foods such as white bread, bagels
and croissants are made from white flour, meaning that all the
nutrition, fibre and essential oils have been stripped out of the
original grain. This makes them easy to digest and results in a
high Gi rating – in other words, most baked goods are red light.

What we are looking for are baked goods made from 100
per cent wholemeal flour and whole grains. If the flour is

stoneground, so much the better. With bread, we are looking for at least 2.5–3g of fibre per slice. Check your labels, because that apparently wholesome-looking seven-grain bread may well list as its principal ingredient unbleached or enriched white flour. The seven grains are mere decoration.

Crispbreads (high fibre)
100% stoneground wholemeal bread
Wholegrain high-fibre bread (2.5–3g of fibre per slice)

For a complete list of red, yellow and green light bakery products see appendix 1 page 134.

FISH COUNTER

All fish and shellfish are green light. Deep-sea fish such as salmon and cod are rich in omega-3 oils, which are great for heart and health. Fish should not be battered or breaded. Go to page 85 for the chance to savour many delicious seafood recipes. Remember, your serving size should be 125g (4oz), or the size of the palm of your hand.

Fish
All fresh fish
All frozen fish
Caviar
Fish tinned in water
Pickled herring
Sashimi
Smoked fish
Squid

Shellfish
Clams (tinned or fresh)
Crab (tinned or fresh)
Lobster (tinned or fresh)
Prawns (tinned or fresh)
Oysters (fresh or smoked)
Scallops
Scampi

For a complete list of red, yellow and green light fish and shellfish see appendix 1 page 132.

MEAT COUNTER

Most meats contain saturated fat. Some of this can be removed by trimming visible fat but the rest is inherent in the meat. Therefore, it's important to select cuts of meats that are intrinsically lean, such as round or loin cuts. Skinless chicken or turkey breasts are the low-fat benchmark.

Other top non-meat choices, whether you are a vegetarian or not, are tofu, Quorn and soy-based TVP (textured vegetable protein), which are low in saturated fat and high in protein. Again, remember your serving size must not exceed 125g (4oz).

Beef
Extra-lean minced steak
Eye round
Top round

Pork
Back bacon
Lean ham
Tenderloin

Poultry
Chicken breast (skinless)
Turkey breast (skinless)

Veal
Chops on the bone
Cutlets
Loin chop
Rib roast
Shank

Other
Ostrich
Rabbit
Venison

For a complete list of red, yellow and green light meats see appendix 1 page 132.

TINNED BEANS/VEGETABLES AISLE

Beans/legumes are the perfect green light food, high in protein and fibre yet low in fat. Unfortunately, tinned beans have a higher Gi than dried beans because of the high temperatures used in the canning process to avoid spoilage. They are, however, very convenient. Tinned beans with added meat, sugar or molasses should be avoided. It's always preferable to buy fresh or frozen vegetables rather than tinned and is more economical if you buy them in large family-sized packs.

Dried beans
Black beans
Black-eyed peas

Butter beans
Chickpeas
Haricots
Kidney beans
Lentils
Mung
Soybeans
Split peas

Tinned beans
Baked beans (low fat)
Black beans
Black-eyed peas
Butter beans
Cannellini beans (white)
Chickpeas
Haricots
Kidney beans (red)
Lentils
Mung
Pigeon beans
Soybeans
Roasted red peppers
Tinned tomatoes
Tomato purée

For a complete list of red, yellow and green light tinned beans and vegetables see appendix 1 page 132.

PASTA AND SAUCES AISLE

Most pastas (other than tinned) are green light, in particular wholewheat versions. Always undercook – *al dente* – with some firmness to the bite. Serving size is important here. Aim for 40g (1½ oz) dry weight, and use pasta as a side-dish starter, not as the basis of your meal.

Choose sauces that are preferably low-sugar (light). Tomato sauce is rich in Lycopene, which has been shown to reduce the risk of prostate cancer.

Pasta
Capellini
Fettuccine
Linguine
Macaroni
Penne
Rigatoni
Spaghetti
Vermicelli

Pasta sauces
Healthy Choice pasta sauces
Light sauces with vegetables (no added sugar)

For a complete list of red, yellow and green light pastas and pasta sauces see appendix 1 page 132.

TINNED SOUP/SEAFOOD/MEAT AISLE
Tinned foods have a higher Gi rating than those that are fresh or cooked from scratch, but they are very convenient when time is limited. Soups are good 'fillers' and help moderate the amount you eat during the rest of the meal. Chunky vegetable soups are the best choice – avoid cream and puréed soups.

Soup
Baxter's Healthy choice
Bouillon (low sodium)

Tinned low-fat bean and vegetable soups
Miso soup

For a complete list of red, yellow and green light canned soup see appendix 1 page 132.

GRAINS

Many whole grains, with all the nutrition and fibre intact, are green light. When it comes to rice, choose long grain as it has a much lower Gi than sticky or glutinous short grain rice (the sort found in Chinese restaurants or in Italian risotto rice).

Barley
Buckwheat
Bulgur
Flaxseeds
Long grain rice (basmati, brown and wild)
Quinoa
Wheat berries

For a complete list of red, yellow and green light grains see appendix 1 page 132.

INTERNATIONAL FOOD AISLE

There are many flavourful foods and sauces from all over the world to choose from here.

Asian
Buckwheat noodles
Bamboo shoots (tinned)
Water chestnuts (tinned)

Cellophane (mung bean) noodles
Chilli sauce
Curry paste
Dried seaweed
Hoisin sauce
Hot chilli paste
Miso
Pickled ginger
Rice vinegar
Soy sauce (low sodium)
Teriyaki sauce
Wasabi

Mexican
Chipotle en adobo (jalapeno peppers in adobo sauce)
Green chillis (tinned)
Pickled jalapenos
Salsa (no added sugar)
Taco sauce (no added sugar)

Middle eastern
Falafel mix
Hummus
Tahini

For a complete list of red, yellow and green light
international foods see appendix 1 page 132.

OIL/VINEGAR/SALAD DRESSING/PICKLES AISLE
Top choices for cooking oils are olive, rapeseed (canola)
and flax.

Dressings should be low fat. However, as acid slows
down the digestive process, thereby reducing the meal's

Gi, vinaigrettes are a best buy. Even better, make your own vinaigrette just by mixing olive oil and balsamic vinegar.

Many condiments and pickles are low Gi. Check labels for those with sugar or other natural sweeteners such as ketchup and brown sauce, which are not recommended.

Cooking oil
Extra virgin olive oil
Flax oil
Olive oil
Rapeseed oil
Safflower oil
Vegetable oil
Vegetable oil spray

Vinegar
Balsamic vinegar
Cider vinegar
Red wine vinegar
Rice vinegar
White vinegar
White wine vinegar

Salad dressings
Low-fat, low-sugar salad dressings
Low-fat, low-sugar vinaigrettes

Pickles
Capers
Cocktail onions
Dill pickles
Olives
Pickled hot peppers
Pickled mixed vegetables

Pickled mushrooms
Sauerkraut

Condiments
Chilli sauce
Cocktail sauce
Dijon mustard
Gravy mix (maximum 20 calories per 120ml [4fl.oz] serving)
Horseradish
Mayonnaise (fat free/reduced fat)
Mustard
Salsa (no added sugar)
Seafood
Steak sauce
Tabasco
Teriyaki sauce
Worcestershire sauce

For a complete list of red, yellow and green light oil/vinegar/
salad dressing/pickles see appendix 1 page 132.

SNACKS AISLE

Snacks are an important part of the Gi Diet. There are many
red light temptations here, so check the green light list below
carefully, in particular so-called 'nutrition' or 'food' bars. Most
are cereal and sugar based with little nutritional value. The
ones to look for should contain at least 10–15g of protein and
around 5g of fat per 50–60g bar. A serving is half a bar. Slim
Fast is a good choice.

Almonds
Cashews
Food bars (see above)

Hazelnuts
Macadamia nuts
Pistachios
Pumpkin seeds
Salsa (no added sugar)
Soya nuts
Sugar-free boiled sweets
Sunflower seeds
Tinned fruit salad
Tinned mandarin oranges
Tinned peaches in juice or water
Tinned pears in juice or water

For a complete list of red, yellow and green light snacks see appendix 1 page 132.

BAKING AISLE

While commercial baked goods are almost all red light, you can make your own sweet treats using the recipes on pages 57–124, as well as from my other books – *The Gi Diet*, *Living the Gi Diet*, and *The Gi Diet Green Light Cookbook*. End of commercial! Although dried fruit is generally red or yellow light, a small amount is acceptable to add flavour to your baked dishes. Splenda (sucralose) is derived from sugar without the calories and is our preferred choice for sweetener.

Sweeteners
Aspartame
Hermesetas Gold
Splenda
Stevia
Sweet'N Low

Spices and flavourings
Bouillon (low sodium)
Extracts (vanilla, etc.)
Garlic
Gravy mixes (20 calories maximum per 120ml [4fl oz] serving)
Herbs
Lemon juice
Pepper (fresh ground)
Salt
Seasoning mixes with no added sugar
Spices
Stock (chicken/beef/vegetable)

Baking supplies
Almonds
Baking powder
Bicarbonate of soda
Cinnamon
Cashews
Cocoa
Hazelnuts
Macadamia nuts
Oat bran
Pumpkin seeds
Sunflower seeds
Vanilla extract
Wheat bran
Wheat germ
Wholemeal flour

For a complete list of red, yellow and green light baking products see appendix 1 page 132.

BREAKFAST FOODS

Most cold cereals have a high Gi and are red light as they are made principally from highly processed grains with the nutrition and fibre removed. These include so-called 'natural' or 'healthy' granola-type cereals as they are high in sugar and low in fibre. Also avoid cereal bars (see 'Snacks' page 37).

Look for cold cereals that have at least 10g of fibre per serving. They may not be much fun in themselves, but they can be dressed up with nuts, fruit and yogurt.

The king of hot cereals is porridge made with large-flake traditional oats (not instant or quick oats). It takes about three minutes in the microwave. Topped with fruit and nuts, this is absolutely my number one choice for breakfast and something many of you will not have eaten since you were children.

Low-sugar or extra-fruit jams, where fruit is listed as the first ingredient, are terrific for wholemeal toast or for flavouring cereals and low-fat dairy products such as yogurt and cottage cheese.

Cereal
100% bran
All-bran
Bran buds
Fibre 1
Fibre First
Large-flake oatmeal (e.g. Jordan's)
Oat bran
Steel-cut oatmeal

Spreads and jams
Extra fruit spreads or jams (no added sugar, fruit as first ingredient)

For a complete list of red, yellow and green light breakfast foods see appendix 1 page 132.

BEVERAGE AISLE

You need to drink up to eight glasses of liquid per day to keep your body hydrated and healthy. We recommend a glass of water before every meal. Having your stomach partly filled with liquid makes you feel full more quickly, thus reducing the temptation to overeat.

Drinks with caffeine, such as coffee, tend to stimulate the appetite and are therefore red light. The exception is tea, containing half the caffeine of coffee, which is acceptable in moderation and is a good source of flavonoids (antioxidants), which are beneficial for heart health. Decaf coffee is a good idea – the latest brands taste like the real thing.

With regards to fruit or vegetable juice, it is better to eat the original fruit or vegetable than drink the juice. The fruit or vegetable has a lower Gi, less calories and more nutrients. An excellent choice is skimmed milk – try to drink a glass a day as a snack or in lieu of water at meal times. Light, plain soya milk is a great alternative.

Bottled water (sparkling or still)
Decaffeinated coffee
Diet soft drinks (without caffeine)
Herbal teas
Iced tea (with no added sugar)
Light instant chocolate
Tea (with or without caffeine)

For a complete list of red, yellow and green light beverages see appendix 1 page 132.

DAIRY CABINET

Low-fat dairy products are a Gi diet staple. They are rich in protein, calcium and vitamin D. Regular or full-fat dairy foods are not recommended as they are loaded with saturated fat. Butter and cheese are among the principal villains. However, you can use small amounts of full-flavoured cheeses as a flavour enhancer when sprinkled lightly on salads, omelettes and pasta. There are some excellent new ultra low-fat cheeses that are acceptable.

Fruit-flavoured, fat-free yogurts with sweetener are ideal for adding to breakfast cereals, as a snack or as a topping for a fruit desert. If you are lactose intolerant, soya milk is an increasingly popular choice. Look for plain, low-fat versions, as the flavoured ones can contain high levels of sugar.

Milk
Buttermilk
Skimmed milk
Soya milk (plain, low-fat)

Cheese
Cheese (fat-free)
Cottage cheese (1% or fat-free)
Extra low-fat cheese (e.g. Laughing Cow light, Boursin light)
Low-fat soya cheese

Yogurt and sour cream
Crème fraîche
Fruit yogurt (non-fat with sugar substitute)
Sour cream (non-fat/reduced sugar)

Butter and margarine
Soft margarine (nonhydrogenated light)

Eggs
Egg whites

Omega-3 eggs

For a complete list of red, yellow and green light dairy products see appendix 1 page 132.

FROZEN FOOD SECTION

Almost all the prepared meals found in the frozen food section of your supermarket are red light because of the ingredients used and the way in which they are processed. They are, however, very convenient and if you are really pushed for time, you might want to keep a couple of prepared meals on hand for emergencies. Your best choices are the 'healthy' brands such as Tesco's 'Healthy Living', Sainsbury's 'Be Good to Yourself' and Marks & Spencer's 'Count on Us'. They are, however, usually light on vegetables so always add a portion or two of a vegetable or a side salad.

The freezer section is a great source of convenient and time-saving green light foods. Frozen vegetables, fruit and fish are all ideal green light choices. Just make sure vegetables aren't in a butter, cream or cheese sauce and the fish is not battered or breaded. The family-size large packs of fruit and vegetables are a particularly good buy.

Vegetables
Asparagus
Beans (green/runner)
Broccoli
Brussels sprouts
Carrots
Cauliflower
Okra
Peas

Peppers
Spinach

Prepared foods
Chicken souvlaki
Extra-lean burgers
Frozen fish without breaded coating
Quorn
Scallops and prawns without breaded coating
Textured vegetable protein
Tofu
Veggie burgers

Desserts
Frozen soya desserts with less than 100 calories per 120g (4oz)
Ice cream (low-fat and no added sugar)

Fruit
Blackberries
Blueberries
Cherries
Cranberries
Peaches
Raspberries
Rhubarb
Strawberries
Summer fruits

For a complete list of red, yellow and green light frozen foods see appendix 1 page 132.

TIME SAVERS

Supermarkets have long recognised that many people have limited time to cook, and there is now an abundance of prepared and frozen foods available. With careful shopping, you can serve delicious green light meals with minimal effort. We have scanned all the major supermarket chains in the UK and looked for items that don't need chopping or can go straight into the pot or pan. They may cost a little more, but they are invaluable if you need to save on preparation time.

Most major supermarkets carry the following
Pre-cooked and sliced chicken breast fillets in various
    flavours but without sauce, e.g. chicken tikka, chicken
    Thai, chicken barbecue, etc.
Prepared fish fillets or steaks, e.g. salmon – without sauce
Prepared seafood, e.g. prawns – without sauce
Packages of pre-cut fresh vegetables, including mixed
    vegetables suitable for stir-fry
Packaged and pre-washed salad greens – many varieties

In the freezer look for
Chopped/crushed garlic cubes
Chopped fresh herbs – parsley, dill, coriander, basil
Crushed ginger
Diced onions
Sliced mixed vegetables e.g. Mediterranean mix, farmhouse
    mix and individual packages of cut vegetables
Frozen berries
Quorn products

Vegetable/Chicken/Beef Stock
Many recipes call for stock, but you don't need to go to the trouble of making it yourself. Where possible, use a liquid stock. You can find fresh stock in 250ml pots in the chiller cabinet, or use a quality bouillon powder (e.g. Marigold) or cube.

CHAPTER 4: INTRODUCTION TO GREEN LIGHT COOKING

The notion of going on a diet can be daunting. People are often fearful that their food choices will be limited to unappetising, bland dishes that are tricky to prepare. This is definitely not the case with the Gi Diet! You can eat very well on the Gi Diet and never have to sacrifice flavour or convenience. Not only are green light foods high in fibre, and low in saturated fat and sugar, but they are also some of the best-tasting foods around. Extra virgin olive oil, for example, is a monosaturated or 'best' fat, and adds a wonderfully robust flavour to many dishes.

The key points with these recipes are that they are:

- Green light

- Easy and quick to prepare

- Taste delicious

Here are some tips on ingredients, equipment and side dishes. You'll also find helpful advice on food preparation and cooking throughout the recipes.

INGREDIENTS

You will notice that not all of the ingredients in the recipes are strictly green light. Occasionally I have added wine for depth of flavour as well as small amounts of sauces that contain sugar and dried fruit. This doesn't mean that the recipe is yellow or red light. The quantities are small enough that they will have little or no effect on your blood-sugar levels, meaning they retain their green light status! To replace sugar in recipes, I use Splenda, a derivative of sugar but without the calories, with great success

– the flavour is excellent. Look for the granular type because it is the easiest to use. Please note, all the major sugar substitutes measure in equal *volume* to sugar, not weight. In other words, one tablespoon of sugar equals one tablespoon of sweetener. To keep it simple we have put all the measurements using sugar substitutes in level tablespoons (15ml).

SIDE DISHES

Almost all the dinner recipes I have included in this book should be accompanied by side dishes, especially salads. We offer some suggestions for side dishes in all our dinner recipes.

PORTIONS

Don't forget, a quarter of your plate should be filled with carbohydrates such as pasta, rice or boiled new potatoes. Since overcooking tends to raise the Gi level of food, boil pasta until it is just *al dente*, and take rice off the heat before it starts to clump together.

Another quarter should contain lean protein – 125g (4oz), or enough to fit in the palm of your hand.

The remaining half of your plate should be filled with green light vegetables and salads. Again, do not overcook the veggies; they should be tender-crisp. Who actually likes mushy vegetables, anyway?

RECIPE SERVINGS

Most of the recipes are devised for two persons, except where indicated. This means they are easily halved for a single serving or doubled when serving four people.

THE EXPRESS KITCHEN

This book has been written for busy people. You may be a working mum or dad rushing home after a long day at work to rustle up dinner, or you could be a single person with a hectic social life. Maybe you're a shift worker or a stay-at-home mum, with small children demanding your full attention. Or perhaps you consider cooking to be something of a chore. Whoever you are and whatever the life you lead, you have decided to eat the healthy green light way but don't have the luxury of endless time on your hands to invest in preparing meals.

The way round this is to prepare the kitchen worksite wisely. A little time spent doing this will reap enormous time-saving benefits later.

THE EQUIPMENT

A microwave oven
I believe microwave ovens were designed to make life easier. They have many more uses than reheating leftovers or thawing frozen meals, even if both are useful functions. Fresh or frozen vegetables can be cooked in minutes, and microwaving often preserves nutrients better than other methods because the cooking time is reduced and little water is used.

When preparing vegetables, leave them in larger pieces, use small amounts of liquid and cover to reduce cooking time. A serving of vegetables for two cooks to *al dente* in about three to five minutes. Fruit crumbles can be prepared in microwaves. They may not brown or crisp, but they will be ready to eat in a few minutes and still taste delicious.

Other equipment
Kitchen scales
Measuring spoons
Good knives and a knife sharpener
Nonstick frying pans – have two of different sizes plus lids, which are really useful, as you can cook with less oil and cleaning up is easy (apply the oil with a light brush or use oil sprays)
Steamer
Tongs – plastic for nonstick pans make lifting, turning and moving foods much easier

Storage containers suitable for freezing

Greaseproof paper for lining trays in ovens – reduces cleaning-up time

Recipe-book holder

Grater – buy the kind that is flat in design and can be held over the pan or bowl so you can grate directly

PLACING THE EQUIPMENT

Besides knowing where everything is, all your equipment must be at arm's reach. This is true in small and large kitchens. Keep your scales on the counter if you have room so you don't have to pull them out each time you use them. Have wooden spoons, tongs and spatulas in a pot next to the stove. Herbs and spices should also be within easy reach.

GETTING READY TO COOK

When you have decided on a recipe, **get all the ingredients out before you start**. Then have to hand the measuring spoons, scales, pots and pans you will need. Do not start cooking until you have done this. It is a waste of time to be running round the kitchen looking for food items and equipment.

COOKING BASICS FOR THE EXPRESS GI DIET

BEANS AND LEGUMES

Beans and lentils are a great source of protein and fibre. For convenience, use canned beans. Just remember to rinse and drain thoroughly before use. Toss a handful of beans such as chickpeas, edamame (fresh soy beans) or cannellini into your soup, salad or stir-fry. Tossing mixed beans with chopped cucumber, tomato, red onion, parsley or coriander and dressing makes a tasty quick salad. Top with cooked chicken or lean ham and you have yourself a meal.

FISH AND SEAFOOD

Fish and seafood can be quick and easy to prepare. Buy fish fresh, frozen or ready prepared and cooked. Just avoid fish that is breaded, fried or in a sauce. The taste of a fillet is easily enhanced or varied by the addition of herbs, fruits and other seasonings. If you haven't the time to prepare a topping, sprinkle on a small amount of dried Herbes de Provence before cooking and top with a squeeze of lemon juice after.

As well as sautéing, fish can be poached, steamed, baked and grilled. Here are approximate cooking times for 125–150g (4–5oz fillets).

Sauté uncovered

Most fish can be sautéed. Season the fillet, then heat one teaspoon of oil in a nonstick frying pan over a medium-high heat. Cook for two to three minutes per side.

Sauté covered

This method keeps the fish very moist. Sauté uncovered for one minute per side as above. Then lower the heat, cover and cook until done, about four to five minutes. The fish will feel firm to the touch and white juices will just start to appear.

Steamed

Cook the fillet over boiling water for about six to eight minutes. When ready the fish will feel firm to touch and white juices will just start to appear.

Grilled

Fish can be cooked under a grill, on an outside grill or in a grill pan. Spray the grill pan with oil, heat and cook the fish for two to three minutes per side. This is great for salmon, tuna and seafood such as prawns.

Microwave

Fish can be cooked quickly in a microwaveable dish, covered in clingfilm (leave a small opening for steam) for about five minutes.

Note: It is important not to overcook fish. Cook until the flesh is opaque and firm but still moist, *and stand for three to five minutes after cooking*. After a while, you will get to know your stove or grill and the times required to cook fish properly.

FRUIT

Fruits make a great snack accompaniment or a sweet dessert. Use canned or frozen fruit (preferably frozen) when local fresh fruits are not available or too expensive. If you're using canned fruit, try to buy it in juice, but if you do buy it in syrup, drain and rinse the fruit before use. Thawed frozen raspberries or summer berries with a little flavoured yogurt make an easy dessert. Toss some frozen berries into your hot porridge or into your muffin mix for added flavour.

GARLIC

Buy one garlic head at a time so the flavour stays fresh. Ready-to-use finely chopped garlic is available at the supermarket in bottles or frozen.

GRAINS

Grains can be an excellent source of protein and fibre, as well as providing essential amino acids. Ground flaxseed can be sprinkled onto porridge or yogurt. While some grains such as barley take almost an hour to cook, some like quinoa and bulgur require less cooking time. Try using it in place of rice for a change in taste and texture.

HERBS AND SPICES

Herbs and spices are an essential element of flavourful cooking, so for express cooking keep dried herbs and seasoning handy. Buy them in small amounts and replace every three to six months. Do not keep them sitting by or on the stove – the heat will destroy the flavour intensity of herbs and spices. Key herbs and spices include: chilli powder, cinnamon, cumin, ginger, basil, bay leaves, Herbes de Provence, oregano, tarragon and thyme. Several herbs are now available in freshly frozen portions in your supermarket.

PASTA

Use wholewheat pastas when possible. For express cooking, put on a pot of water plus a quarter of a teaspoon of salt as soon as you start the recipe (tip – water-heating time can be reduced by bringing water to the boil in an electric kettle). Use 40g (1½ oz) of dry pasta per serving.

POTATOES

Use two to three boiled new or small potatoes per serving. Season with chopped fresh parsley, a little lemon juice and freshly ground pepper.

POULTRY

Skinless, boneless chicken breasts can be prepared quickly and with a minimum of fuss. They can be cooked whole, or flattened as a cutlet. To make a cutlet, place a breast between clingfilm and pound with a rolling pin or mallet until it is about 2cm (¾ in.) thick. Try cutting the breast or cutlet into strips or cubes for super-fast stir-fries. Remember, always cook chicken until it is *no longer pink inside and its juices run clear*. For a whole breast weighing 125–150g (4–5oz) this usually means about six to eight minutes per side. Cutlets, strips or cubes require less time.

Variety is the spice of life, as they say, and there is no reason your chicken dishes can't be as varied and interesting as possible, and we have provided plenty of suggestions for easy-to-make sauces, salsas and seasoning. After you have cooked the chicken, simply use the pan juices as a base for the sauces: add liquid, some seasoning, simmer for a few minutes and serve!

RICE

Use long grain basmati rice and rinse well before using. Put some water or stock on to boil when you begin cooking your recipe, then add your rice and turn down to simmer so the rice is ready when the main recipe has been cooked. Basmati rice takes about ten to twelve minutes to cook. Brown rice, especially brown basmati, is an excellent choice, but it takes longer to cook (around thirty to forty minutes). If you want to use brown rice, factor in the added time – once it's on, you don't have to stir or fuss.

SALADS

Supermarkets sell a wide variety of salad greens ready to use, so there's no need to get bored with the same old salad every day. Varieties include baby spinach, rocket, cos, leafy, crispy and watercress. Add fresh plum tomatoes, sliced cucumber and red onion for a traditional mixed salad. Try adding some beans, for example chickpeas, or other chopped fresh vegetables. Or you could add some sliced or chopped pear and a crumble of blue cheese to baby spinach with white wine vinaigrette for a delicious taste. Other good additions to salad greens are strawberries, blueberries, raspberries, chopped peaches or nectarines. Then toss with a vinaigrette.

SALAD DRESSINGS

There are many low-fat, low-sugar dressings available or, if you have time, make your own. Keep different wine vinegars on hand as well as balsamic vinegar and mix with olive oil, Dijon mustard and fresh pepper for a basic vinaigrette variety. When you're in a real rush, just toss greens with balsamic vinegar and oil and fresh pepper.

SWEETENERS

Despite an intensive disinformation campaign by the sugar lobby, sugar substitutes are completely safe and approved by all major government and health authorities worldwide. If you are sensitive to aspartame, try one of the many alternatives.

The best form to use is granular as it can be measured exactly like sugar, by *volume* and not by *weight*, i.e. one tablespoon of sugar equals one tablespoon of sweetener. Our own preference is for Splenda, which is based on sucralose and is ideal for baking.

VEGETABLES

The Gi Diet places a lot of emphasis on vegetables, which should make up half of your dinner plate. You can use fresh or frozen vegetables – the nutrients are the same. Frozen vegetables are usually chopped or cut and ready for use, and supermarkets also sell prepared packages of vegetables ready for stir-fries or steaming, all of which will save you valuable time.

Vegetables can be prepared in many ways.

Microwave

A microwave is a great time-saver. Prepare vegetables into serving pieces, add a small amount of water, cover and cook on high. Two servings of most vegetables will cook in about three to five minutes on a high setting. Cook until the vegetables are done but still crunchy.

Steaming

Heat 3–5cm (1–2in.) of water in a large covered pot. Place your vegetables in a steamer basket, cover and cook for a few minutes. Check the vegetables regularly to make sure they're still crunchy. This is a great method for asparagus, green beans and mixed vegetables.

Stir-fry

Prepare the vegetables in bite- or small-size pieces. Spray with a vegetable oil or heat one teaspoon of olive oil in a nonstick wok or frying pan. Stir-fry the vegetables for a couple of minutes, add finely chopped garlic and/or ginger, and a small amount of fluid such as soy sauce or lemon, then continue cooking for a few minutes until the vegetables are done. Toss in cooked chicken, turkey, prawns, firm tofu or lean ham – try different combinations.

This is a great method for peppers, mushrooms, courgettes, sugar-snap peas and mangetout.

Various greens can be quickly stir-fried. These include spinach and baby bok choy. Cook until they are wilted and the stem parts are tender but not soggy.

Grilling

To grill vegetables, cut to chunk sizes and toss in a small plastic bag with a little olive oil, chopped garlic, ground pepper and soy sauce if desired. Grilling is great for sliced flat-top mushrooms, courgettes, aubergine slices, asparagus, peppers and red onions.

CHAPTER 5: PHASE ONE: LOSING WEIGHT

Having cleared out and restocked your pantry, fridge and freezer with green light foods, and decided how much weight you want to lose, you are now ready to start Phase One, the weight loss phase.

We will start logically with breakfast and work through the day covering lunch, dinner and snacks, offering recipe and meal suggestions along the way. We have also included several of the most popular recipes from our earlier books, adapted to meet the important criteria of being quick to prepare (from start to table in under thirty minutes).

BREAKFAST

This is the most important meal of the day for three reasons. First, you probably haven't eaten for ten to twelve hours and the cornerstone of the Gi Diet is to keep your blood-sugar levels constant and your tummy busy during your waking hours. Second, you will almost certainly overcompensate for a missed breakfast by overeating for the rest of the day. Third, a green light breakfast will make you feel light, energetic, well fed and ready to tackle the day.

For breakfast you have three options depending on your time availability:

- On the run (ten minutes, start to finish)
- Sit down (ten to twenty minutes)
- Brunch/weekends (twenty minutes plus)

'A good breakfast will give you the energy to face the day ahead'

ON THE RUN

If time is of the essence, your best bets are these:

BRAN-DELICIOUS CEREAL

While most high-fibre cold cereals (those with 10g of fibre or more per serving) made with skimmed milk are not a lot of fun for most people, they can easily be livened up.

Here is a popular blend:
Serves 2
Combine:
90g (3oz) All Bran or Bran Flakes
320g (11oz) fresh fruit
250ml (8fl.oz) fruit-flavoured fat-free yogurt with sweetener
4tbsp flaked almonds

MUESLI

Virtually all store-bought muesli is a dietary disaster, packed with sugar, fat and highly processed grains. You can easily make your own green light version in bulk in advance for a yummy fast start to your day.

300g (10oz) jumbo porridge oats
40g (1½ oz) oat bran
40g (1½ oz) flaked almonds
75g (2½ oz) sunflower seeds
2tbsp wheat germ
¼ tsp ground cinnamon

1. Place the oats, oat bran, almonds, sunflower seeds, wheat germ and cinnamon in a large resealable plastic bag. Shake the bag to combine the mixture.

2. Makes about 450g (1lb) (about 7 servings)

3. Storage: Keep in resealable bag or airtight container at room temperature for up to a month.

To use: Mix together 90g (3oz) muesli with 90ml (3fl.oz) milk or water. Cover and chill overnight. In the morning, combine with a container of non-fat fruit yogurt with sweetener and enjoy cold or pop in the microwave for a hot breakfast.

PORRIDGE

Porridge is made with large-flake oats and either water or skimmed milk, and takes only three minutes to prepare in the microwave. Add fruit, yogurt and almonds for a delicious breakfast.

Combine porridge with:
Fresh/frozen/canned fruit
Fat-free fruit yogurt with sweetener
Flaked almonds/ground flaxseed

Your cereal and topping should be sufficient to fill you, but if not, increase your cereal serving size or add a slice of 100 per cent wholemeal toast, a pat of light non-hydrogenated margarine and 'no sugar added' jam (where fruit is listed as the first ingredient).

YOGURT FRUIT SMOOTHIES

While I'm not a big fan of smoothies, as the blending process used to make them raises their Gi, they do offer a healthy alternative for an occasional quick breakfast.

Serves 2
450ml (15fl.oz) skimmed milk
175g (6oz) fruit-flavoured fat-free yogurt with sweetener.
½ tsp sweetener
225g (8oz) fresh or frozen berries

Place all the ingredients in a blender, food processor or smoothie maker and process until smooth.

Tea/Decaf Coffee

Coffee is out in Phase One as caffeine increases appetite. Your best bet is tea or decaf coffee with skimmed milk and no sugar. If life is completely impossible without your jolt of high caffeine, go for it – but limit it to one cup per day.

SIT DOWN

On some weekday mornings and hopefully on the weekend you have extra time to prepare, cook and eat a broader range of foods. Most popular choices are egg-based.

Omelettes or scrambled eggs are easy to make and you can vary them by adding any number of fresh vegetables, a little cheese and/or some meat. You'll find ingredients for a basic omelette here, along with suggestions for making Italian, Mexican, vegetarian and Western versions. But you don't need to stop at these – using the proportions as a guide, you can add whatever green light ingredients strike your fancy. To round off the meal, include some fresh fruit, a glass of skimmed milk or a small fat-free yogurt with sweetener.

BASIC OMELETTE (SINGLE SERVING)

1 egg and 2 egg whites
4tbsp skimmed milk
Vegetables of choice – e.g. mushrooms, peppers, broccoli, onions – sliced

1. Spray some oil in a small nonstick frying pan, and then place it over a medium heat.

2. Add the vegetables and sauté until tender, about 5 minutes. Transfer the sautéed vegetables to a plate and cover with aluminium foil to keep warm.

3. Beat the eggs with the milk and pour them into the frying pan over a medium heat. Cook until the eggs start to firm up, then spread the appropriate vegetables, cheese, herbs, beans and/or meat over them. Continue cooking until the eggs are done to your liking.

For Scrambled Eggs: make scrambled eggs by stirring the eggs as they cook, adding any additional ingredients while the eggs are still soft.

VARIATIONS

Western
To the basic omelette recipe, add:
2 slices back bacon, lean ham or turkey breast, chopped
1 onion, chopped
125g (4oz) chopped red and green peppers
Spices to taste

Vegetarian
To the basic omelette recipe, add:
25g (1oz) grated reduced-fat cheese
50g (1¾ oz) broccoli florets
50g (1¾ oz) sliced mushrooms
50g (1¾ oz) chopped red and green peppers

Italian
To the basic omelette recipe, add:
25g (1oz) grated reduced-fat mozzarella cheese
90g (3oz) sliced mushrooms
125ml (4fl.oz) tomato purée
Fresh or dried herbs to taste, e.g. oregano or basil

SMOKED SALMON SCRAMBLED EGGS

Makes scrambled eggs special. Serve with a slice of high-fibre toast.

Serves 2

3 eggs and 2 egg whites
2tbsp skimmed milk
1tsp vegetable oil
50g (1¾ oz) smoked salmon, chopped
¼ tsp pepper
1tbsp chopped fresh chives or dill

1. In a bowl, whisk together the egg, milk and pepper.

2. In a nonstick frying pan, heat the oil over a medium heat. Add the eggs and, using a rubber spatula, gently stir until the eggs are almost set. Stir in the salmon and continue to cook, stirring gently, until the eggs are set but still slightly creamy. Stir in the chives.

WEEKEND/BRUNCH

Leisurely brunches fall somewhat outside the remit of this book, but if you have time for this luxury, you can find some delicious easy recipes in my illustrated *Gi Diet Green Light Cookbook*. These include: Baked Eggs in Ham Cups, Crustless Quiche and Berry Stuffed French Toast. This will also give you a chance to introduce other members of the family or friends to eating the green light way.

LUNCH

For many people, lunch is one meal that is eaten away from home. This poses two challenges. First, what facilities exist for eating out or buying a take-out in your work neighbourhood, and second, how much time do you have? Let's deal with each in turn.

BRINGING LUNCH TO THE WORKPLACE

This usually means taking a packed lunch to eat at your desk. You will save time by not having to go out, queue and wait to be served, etc. This also has the advantage of making sure you are completely in control of what you eat. The main downside to this is that you need to set aside time to prepare food at home, though this can be more than offset by the time you will save lunching in at work.

The packed lunches we suggest are simple and uncomplicated, and require minimal preparation. Most can be done the night before and put in the fridge. They have been grouped into three popular categories of packed lunches: sandwiches, salads and pasta. I've also added a fast fruit and dairy option when you're really pressed for time. The suggestions assume a fridge is available at work for food storage.

SANDWICHES

The reason sandwiches are probably the most popular international lunch is that they are easy to make, portable and have endless variations. Here are some guidelines to make your sandwich into a convenient and filling green light meal.

- Always use stoneground 100 per cent wholemeal or high-fibre bread (2.5–3g of fibre per slice)
- During Phase One, sandwiches should be eaten open-faced, in order to keep to the recommendation one slice/serving.

- Include at least three vegetables, such as lettuce, tomato, red and green peppers, cucumber, bean sprouts or onion
- Use mustard or hummus as a spread on the bread (no regular mayonnaise or butter)
- Add 120g (4oz) of cooked lean meat or fish
- Mix tinned tuna or chopped, cooked chicken with low-fat mayonnaise/salad dressing and celery
- Mixed tinned salmon with malt vinegar
- To help sandwiches stay fresh, not soggy, pack components separately and assemble them just before eating, if possible – buy two or three reusable containers, including a small container for dressing

If it's not convenient to bring your own then there are some excellent green light buys, for example from four of the most popular sandwich shops/supermarkets:

- Tesco/Tesco Express: 'Healthy Living' sandwiches
- Sainsbury's: 'Be Good to Yourself' sandwiches
- Marks & Spencers: 'Count on Us' sandwiches
- Prêt a Manger: 'Slim Prêt' sandwiches
- It's a good idea to add a green salad to your sandwich (available in most of these stores), and if possible, without making too much of a mess of the sandwich and your lap, eat open-faced.

SALADS

Here is a basic salad to which you can add your choice of protein; tinned tuna/salmon, sliced cooked chicken breast, lean deli ham, tofu or beans.

BASIC SALAD

40g (1½oz) torn or coarsely salad greens, such as cos, rocket, iceberg lettuce, mesclun, or watercress
1 small carrot, grated
½ red, yellow, or green pepper, chopped
1 plum tomato, cut into wedges
90g (3oz) cucumber, sliced
30g (1¼oz) red onion, sliced, optional
Basic Vinaigrette (see below)

1. Place the lettuce and/or greens, carrot, pepper, tomato, cucumber and onion, if using, in a bowl and toss to mix. Pour about 1 tablespoon of the vinaigrette over the salad and toss to mix.

2. For lunch at the office, pack greens and vegetables in one container and dressing in another. Mix at lunchtime.
Makes 1 serving

BASIC VINAIGRETTE

2tbsp balsamic vinegar
1tsp Dijon mustard
1tsp dried basil
1/2 tsp sugar substitute
1/2 tsp salt
Pinch of freshly ground pepper
4tbsp extra virgin olive oil

1. In a bowl, whisk together the vinegar, mustard, basil, sugar substitute, salt and pepper. Gradually whisk in the oil.

2. Makes about 120ml (4fl.oz) of dressing. The dressing will keep in the fridge for 1 week.

3. Use 1 tablespoon of dressing per portion of greens.

Tip: This vinaigrette is good tossed with halved cherry tomatoes, cooked green beans or asparagus.

PASTA

Cook extra pasta at dinnertime and use it as the basis for a lunch or two. It will keep fresh in the fridge for several days. This is a great time-saver. Here is a basic pasta salad for lunch or dinner.

BASIC PASTA SALAD

40g (1½ oz) uncooked wholewheat pasta (spirals, shells, or similar shape)

150g (5oz) chopped, cooked vegetables (such as broccoli, asparagus, bell peppers, or scallions)

3tbsp light tomato sauce or other low-fat or non-fat pasta sauce

125g (4oz) chopped cooked chicken or other lean meat, such as ground lean turkey or lean chicken sausage

Prepare the pasta and cool. Place the pasta, vegetables, tomato sauce and chicken in a bowl and stir to mix well. Chill the salad, covered, until ready to use, then heat it in the microwave or serve chilled.

Makes 1 serving

Variation: You can use the proportions here as a guide and vary the vegetables, sauce, and source of protein to suit your tastes and add variety to your pasta salad lunches.

ON THE RUN

Here are two fast and filling green light options for occasional use when you are really pushed for time.

COTTAGE CHEESE AND FRUIT

1x200g tub low-fat cottage cheese
180g (6oz) chopped, fresh or canned fruit in juice, e.g. peaches,
   apricots or pears

Place the cottage cheese and fruit in a plastic bowl with
a fitted lid and stir to mix. Store in the refrigerator until
lunchtime. Enjoy.
Makes 1 serving

*Add half a nutrition bar, such as a Slim Fast Meal Bar, and you're
on your way in minutes.*

EGG AND VEG

1 hard-boiled egg
About 100g (3 ½ oz) prepared cut veggies
2tbsp hummus
1 slice high-fibre bread or crispbreads

Hard boil an egg and leave it in its shell to transport it easily
to the office. Prepare a bag of cut raw veggies e.g. broccoli or
cauliflower florets, cucumber slices, small cherry tomatoes,
small carrots, sliced peppers, or buy ready prepared veggies and
keep on hand in refrigerator. Pack egg, veggies, some hummus
and bread in separate bags or small containers.
Makes 1 serving

EATING OUT

SANDWICHES

If you really don't have time to prepare a lunch box, a green light takeaway sandwich is your best bet. Try to make sure it has:

- 100 per cent wholemeal bread
- Hummus or mustard in lieu of butter, margarine or mayo
- Slices of chicken/turkey breast, ham or tuna – avoid mayo, cheese and bacon bits
- Lots of vegetables – tomatoes, lettuce, peppers, onion rings, bean sprouts, etc.
- Always remove the top slice of bread and eat open-faced.

FAST FOOD

Another option if time presses is, believe it or not, a fast-food restaurant. Several of the leading chains have introduced menu items that are lower in fat and calories. A word of caution, however – a substantial amount of sodium (salt) is often added to offset any perceived flavour loss. A principal villain is the salad dressing, so only use half the sachet. Just be aware of the minefield of red light temptations!

Here are some green light offerings in five of the major fast-food/take-out food chains.

McDonald's

McDonald's is the grandfather (or godfather?) of the fast-food industry with the largest worldwide sales. With products such as the 'quarter pounder' and large fries weighing in at 970 calories and 47g of fat, they have not surprisingly become the favourite target for nutritionists and other health activists.

McDonald's has, however, made a tentative start to changing their dietary catastrophe, though it is still only a nominal part of their overall menu. Here are your best green light options:

Sandwiches
Chicken tikka toasted deli sandwich (brown roll)
Chicken salad toasted deli sandwich (brown roll)

Salads
Grilled chicken ranch salad

Dressings
Newman's balsamic

Snacks
Carrot sticks
Fruit bag

Burger King
Burger King is the last of the major burger chains to enter the lower-fat market. Still, better late than never – I hope they'll be encouraged to broaden their offerings. Suffice to say that with their flagship Whopper and fries weighing in at 1,117 calories with a mind- and artery-numbing 58g of fat, they clearly have a lot to make up for.

Here are their best green light options:

Sandwiches
Spicy Piri Piri chicken baguette
Flame-grilled chicken sandwich

Salads
Flame-grilled chicken salad
Warm crispy chicken salad

Dressings
French dressing
Tomato and basil dressing

Subway

Subway is to be congratulated as the pacesetters in the fast-food industry with its broad range of low-fat products. They deserve a Gi Diet gold star and warrant your support.

Sandwiches ('6 inch under 6g subs')
Roast beef
Roast chicken breast
Subway club
Turkey breast
Turkey breast and ham
Veggie Delite

Deli subs
Ham Deli
Roast Beef Deli
Turkey Breast Deli
Note: the best choice in 6-inch rolls are Italian or Wheat.

Salads
Grilled chicken
Subway Club
Veggie Delite

Wraps:
Turkey breast

Sauces
Honey Mustard
Sweet Onion
Bacon

Prêt a Manger

Only a couple of years ago, I wrote in the first edition of my pocket guide to shopping and eating out that Prêt a Manger should be avoided because of their high fat menu. Since then there has been a dramatic sea shift with the introduction of a line of green light sandwiches that I can heartily recommend.

Slim Pret Sandwiches
BLT
Chicken avocado
Chicken Caesar
Classic tuna
Crayfish and rocket
Hummus salad
Superclub

Salads
Chicken tabbouleh and yogurt salad bowl
Crayfish and smoked salmon salad bowl
New tuna salad bowl
No-bread chicken Provencal
No-bread tabbouleh

Pizza Hut

Whereas I recommend avoiding pizza restaurants like the plague, I am delighted to see that Pizza Hut has made a real effort to introduce a line of pizzas and other foods that meet the green light criteria. Let's hope the rest of their competition follows their admirable lead.

Salads
Warm Chicken Salad
Salad Bar: tomato and basil pesto salad – fresh vegetables are your best choices

Pizza (two slices per serving)
Individual Hi-Light Vegetarian
Individual Hi-Light Chicken
Individual Hi-Light Ham
Dressing
Oil-free vinaigrette

Other Fast Food

From here it is all downhill. Even Pizza Express's Salad Niçoise, where you might expect a glimmer of green light, has an astonishing 49g of fat (your entire daily fat intake) and 827 calories!

Similarly, avoid KFC if you value your waistline.

Takeaway

The best advice is, don't eat take-out food except where identified above. The emphasis is on price, convenience and speed, not nutrition. If you must, then Indian is your best bet.

Fish and Chips

The UK's most famous contribution to international cuisine and obesity. A classic example of taking an ideal food, fish, adulterating it with calorie-loaded batter and then deep-frying it in oil. Throw in deep-fried potatoes and you have the making of a nutritional disaster.

Chinese

Not a good choice, because much Chinese food is deep-fried or smothered in sweet or sodium-saturated sauces. However, there are a few opportunities such as dishes that contain steamed or stir-fried vegetables along with chicken, seafood or tofu. Avoid the glutinous or sticky rice and noodles (except for cellophane noodles made from mung beans).

Indian

Probably your best choice, as vegetables, legumes and long grain (basmati) rice are usually predominant. Things to avoid are foods fried in ghee (clarified butter) and anything prepared in creamy sauces. Baked or grilled dishes are your best bet.

Pizza

Don't.

RESTAURANTS

If you have time for a working lunch in a restaurant, there are a few simple rules that will help keep you in the green light zone. Eating out on the Gi Diet is easier than ever. Today, there is a trend for restaurants to use vegetable oils, especially olive oil; there is more emphasis on broiling or grilling rather than frying; a greater variety of vegetables and increased salad options; and more fish dishes are on offer. These all make it even easier to dine out the green light way.

'Follow a few simple rules for restaurant dining to stay in the green light zone'

As dining out is often a social occasion, you want to be able to enjoy yourself with your friends and not feel that you are putting a damper on the occasion. So here are my top ten suggestions:

1. **Don't go to lunch starving.** Make sure you have a substantial mid-morning snack before you go (see snacks, page 119). This will help reduce the temptation to overeat.

2. **Drink water.** On arrival, drink a glass of water.

3. **Bread basket.** Once the habitual basket of rolls or bread has been passed round, which you ignore, with your co-diner's approval, ask the waiter to remove whatever is left in the basket. The longer it sits there, the more tempted you will be to dig in.

4. **Soup/salad.** Order soup or salad first and tell the waiter you would like this as soon as possible. This will stop you sitting there hungry while others are filling up on the bread. For soups, go for vegetable or bean based, the chunkier the better. Avoid cream-based soups. For salads, the golden rule is dressing on the *side* as you will only use a fraction of what the restaurant would smother on. And please avoid Caesar salads, which come pre-dressed.

5. **Double vegetables.** As you probably won't get boiled new potatoes and can't be sure what type of rice is being served, ask for double vegetables instead. I have yet to find a restaurant that won't willingly oblige.

6. **Meat, poultry, seafood: best options.** Stick with low-fat cuts of meat (see shopping guide page 24) or poultry – if necessary, you can remove the skin. Fish and shellfish are an excellent choice but must not be breaded or battered. Remember, servings tend to be generous in restaurants, so eat only about 125–180g (4–6oz) – about the size of a pack of cards – and leave the rest.

7. **Sauces on side.** As with salads, ask for any sauces to be put on the side.

8. **Avoid desserts.** Desserts are a nutritional minefield, with few green light choices on the whole. Fresh fruit and berries, if available, are your best choice, without the ice cream. Most other choices are a dietary disaster. My best advice is to try and avoid dessert. If social pressure becomes overwhelming or it is a special occasion, ask for extra forks so dessert can be shared. A couple of forkfuls with your coffee should get you off the hook with minimal dietary damage!

9. **Decaf coffee.** Only order decaffeinated coffee. Skim decaf cappuccino is our family's favourite.

10. **Eat slowly.** Finally, and perhaps most importantly, eat slowly. In the eighteenth century, the famous Dr Johnson reportedly advised chewing food 32 times before swallowing! That's going a little overboard, but at least put your fork down between mouthfuls. The stomach takes twenty to thirty minutes to let the brain know it feels full. So if you eat quickly, you may be shovelling in more food than you require before the brain says stop. You will also have more time to savour your meal.

DINNER

We normally have a little more time available for dinner. The recipes in this section have been designed to take up to thirty minutes, from start to serving time. You can reduce these times even further – see Cooking Basics, page 49 for some additional time saving ideas.

These recipes are simple and easy to prepare and cook, and have been devised to feed two.

THE RECIPES

Remember to assemble all ingredients and utensils first. Each recipe is accompanied by suggested side orders. If you decide not to include a salad, make sure you add additional vegetables. See 'Cooking Basics for the Express Gi Diet' (page 49) for preparation advice. When these side dishes include rice, potatoes or pasta, the recipe starts with a reminder for you to put water on for these ingredients at the beginning. This way, they will be ready along with the rest of the food.

CHICKEN TARRAGON WITH MUSHROOMS

Tarragon adds a light French flavour. The variation below is great for entertaining.

Prep time **10** minutes   Total time **30** minutes

2 chicken cutlets, about 125g (4oz) each
2tsp vegetable oil
Freshly ground pepper
1tsp non-hydrogenated margarine e.g. Biona or Pure
1 small onion, chopped
225g (8oz) sliced mushrooms
3tbsp vermouth*/white wine

125ml (4fl.oz) chicken stock or water
1tsp dried tarragon

Sides Suggestions (see Basics page 49)
125g (4oz) frozen peas
Basmati rice
Salad greens
White wine vinaigrette

1. Prepare the rice as per Basics instructions. About 2 minutes before the end add the frozen peas, then stir and simmer for 2 minutes.

2. Meanwhile, heat the oil in a nonstick frying pan over a medium-high heat. Sprinkle the chicken with fresh pepper and sauté until done (about 6 minutes per side), then remove to a side dish and cover.

3. In the same pan add margarine and sauté the onion and mushrooms until soft (about 5 minutes), then add the vermouth or wine and tarragon and simmer for 1 minute. Add the stock and simmer for 2 minutes until reduced by half. Season with pepper.

4. Serve the chicken with the rice and pour on the sauce.

Entertaining Variation: This dish can be made with pork escalopes or thin-cut steaks, and instead of adding peas to the rice serve with steamed green beans or asparagus seasoned with a small amount of lemon juice and freshly ground pepper.

vermouth is a great substitute for white wine and stores well

SAUTÉED CHICKEN PROVENCAL

Prep time **10** minutes   Total time **30** minutes

2 skinless, boneless chicken breasts, about 125g (4oz)
1tbsp olive oil
1 clove of garlic, finely chopped
125ml (4fl.oz) chicken stock
1tsp dried Herbes de Provence or mixed herbs
Freshly ground pepper
½ tsp non-hydrogenated margarine
¾ tsp lemon juice

Sides Suggestions (see Basics page 49)
4–6 new potatoes
Mixed vegetables
Tomatoes with balsamic vinegar and olive oil

1. Prepare the potatoes as per Basics instructions.

2. Meanwhile, heat the oil in a nonstick frying pan over a medium-high heat. Sprinkle the chicken with fresh pepper and sauté until done (about 6 minutes per side). Remove to a side dish and cover to keep warm. Meanwhile, prepare the tomato salad.

3. Using the same pan, add the garlic and sauté for 1 minute, stirring constantly. Add the stock and herbs. Simmer the broth until it is reduced by half, then stir in the margarine and lemon juice. Stir for 30 seconds and serve.

ROASTED CHICKEN WITH TOMATOES AND ASPARAGUS

Prep time **5** minutes   Total time **25** minutes

125g (4oz) cherry or grape tomatoes, halved
2tbsp olive oil
3 cloves of garlic, crushed
1tsp dried tarragon
1tsp hot red pepper or dried chilli flakes, or to taste
½ tsp each salt and pepper
2 boneless, skinless chicken breasts
16 asparagus spears, trimmed

Sides Suggestions (see Basics page 49)
Basmati rice
Green salad

1. Prepare the rice as per Basics instructions and preheat the oven to 220°C, Gas 7.

2. Meanwhile, in a large bowl, toss the tomatoes with the olive oil, garlic, tarragon and red pepper flakes.

3. Place the chicken in a shallow ovenproof baking dish. Pour the tomato mixture over the chicken, arranging the tomatoes in a single layer around the chicken. Sprinkle with salt and pepper. Roast in the oven for 20–25 minutes or until the chicken is no longer pink inside.

4. While the chicken cooks, steam the asparagus for 3–4 minutes or until tender-crisp and make your green salad.

5. Transfer the chicken to a platter and spoon the tomatoes and juices over.

CURRIED CHICKEN WITH SNOW PEAS

🕐 Prep time **5** minutes   🕐 Total time **20** minutes

2 skinless, boneless chicken breasts, about 125g (4oz) each, cubed
2tsp olive oil
1 clove of garlic, crushed
1 small onion, chopped
1tsp curry powder or to taste
180g (6fl.oz) chicken stock
125ml (4fl.oz) reduced-fat coconut milk
1 carrot, chopped
¼ tsp salt
Freshly ground pepper
150g (5oz) mangetout or sugar-snap peas

Sides Suggestions (see Basics page 49)
Basmati rice
Mixed-greens salad

1. Prepare the rice as per Basics instructions and heat some water for steaming the mangetout or peas.

2. Meanwhile, heat the oil in a nonstick frying pan over a medium-high heat. Sauté the chicken for about 5 minutes until it's no longer pink inside, then remove to a side dish and keep warm.

3. Add the garlic, onion and curry powder to the pan and cook for 2 minutes until the onions have softened. Add the stock, coconut milk, carrot, salt and pepper; cover and simmer, stirring occasionally, for about 5 minutes. Return the chicken to the pan and simmer uncovered for about 5 minutes. Meanwhile, steam your mangetout or sugar-snap peas for 2–3 minutes (or microwave for 1 minute). Gently stir into the rice and top with the chicken mixture.

QUICK THAI CHICKEN

If you want this curry extra-hot simply increase the curry paste to taste.

Prep time **5** minutes   Total time **30** minutes

2tsp vegetable oil
2tsp Thai red curry paste
250g (9oz) skinless, boneless chicken breasts cut in chunks
1 small onion, sliced
1 red or green pepper, thinly sliced
4tbsp water
4tbsp soured cream or reduced-fat crème fraîche
1tbsp soy sauce
1tsp dried basil

Sides Suggestions (see Basics page 49)
Basmati rice
Green beans
Soft-greens salad topped with chopped mango
Yogurt dressing

1. Prepare the rice as per Basics instructions and prepare your vegetables.

2. Meanwhile, heat the oil in a large nonstick frying pan or wok over a medium-high heat. Add the curry paste and cook for 30 seconds. Add the chicken and stir-fry for 5 minutes. Add the onion and peppers and cook, stirring for about 10 minutes or until the vegetables begin to brown. Add the water, crème fraîche, soy sauce and basil and simmer for 10 minutes or until the chicken is no longer pink inside.

Vegetarian Option: You can use 350g extra-firm tofu, cubed, instead of the chicken.

CHICKEN STIR-FRY

You can use your favourite variation of vegetables for this dish.

Prep time **10** minutes   Total time **25** minutes

1tsp sesame oil
250g (9oz) boneless skinless chicken breasts, chopped
125g (4oz) mushrooms, sliced
1 small onion, chopped
1 clove of garlic, finely chopped
2tsp fresh ginger, grated
1 red pepper, chopped
1 carrot, chopped
1 celery stick, chopped
1tbsp soy sauce
100g (3 1/2 oz) bean sprouts

Sides Suggestions (see Basics page 49)
Basmati rice prepared with chicken stock
Romaine or small cos salad

1. Prepare the rice as per Basics instructions and prepare the salad.

2. Heat the oil in a large nonstick frying pan over a medium-high heat. Cook the chicken, mushrooms, onion, garlic and ginger for about 8 minutes or until the chicken is no longer pink. Add the pepper, carrot, and celery and soy sauce, and cook, stirring for 2 minutes to combine. Add the bean sprouts and toss to combine.

CHICKEN PEPERONATA

2 skinless boneless chicken breasts, about 125g (4oz) each
1tbsp wholemeal flour
2tsp olive oil
1 small onion, sliced
1 clove of garlic, crushed
1 red pepper, thinly sliced
½ yellow or green pepper
1x400g can chopped tomatoes
3tbsp chopped sun-dried tomatoes
½ tsp dried oregano
¼ tsp each salt and pepper

Sides Suggestions (see Basics page 49)
Pasta or rice
Mixed Salad

1. Prepare the pasta or rice as per Basics instructions.

2. Dredge the chicken breasts in flour. Heat the oil in a large nonstick frying pan over a medium-high heat. Add the chicken and brown on both sides, then remove to a plate. Prepare the vegetables.

3. Add the onion and garlic to the frying pan and cook until softened, about 5 minutes. Add the peppers, chopped tomatoes, sun-dried tomatoes, oregano, salt and pepper; bring to the boil. Place the chicken on top of the mixture, then reduce the heat and cook, covered, for 15–20 minutes or until the chicken is no longer pink inside.

SAUTÉED CHICKEN WITH INDIAN RICE

Prep time **5** minutes   Total time **30** minutes

2 skinless, boneless chicken breasts, about 125g (4oz)
Freshly ground pepper
2tsp rapeseed or vegetable oil
1 small onion, chopped
1 clove of garlic, chopped
2tsp garam masala or mild curry powder
100g (3 ½ oz) basmati rice
350ml (12fl.oz) chicken stock

Sides Suggestions (see Basics page 49)
Baby bok choy or Chinese stir-fry vegetable mix

1. Heat 1 teaspoon of oil in a nonstick frying pan over a medium-high heat. Sprinkle the chicken with pepper and cook for 6 minutes per side or until no longer pink inside. Remove to a side dish and cover to keep warm.

2. Heat the remaining oil over a medium heat, then sauté the onion and garlic until softened (about 5 minutes). Stir in the garam masala and cook for 30 seconds. Add the rice, stir and cook for 3 minutes.

3. Stir in the broth and simmer covered for 10–12 minutes until the rice is done. Serve with the chicken breasts.

Variation: This rice is also great with fish. For a vegetarian version of the rice, use vegetable stock.

CHICKEN FINGERS WITH APRICOT-MUSTARD DIPPING SAUCE

Prep time **5** minutes   Total time **15** minutes

(marinade overnight for next day's dinner)

1 egg white
1tbsp soy sauce
1 small clove of garlic, crushed
250g (9oz) skinless, boneless chicken breasts,
    cut in 1cm (½ in.) strips
50g (1¾ oz) toasted sesame seeds*
1tsp rapeseed or vegetable oil
Dipping sauce:
3tbsp low-sugar apricot jam
4tbsp water
1tbsp Dijon mustard

Sides Suggestions (see Basics page 49)
Grilled courgette and aubergine slices
A plate of cut raw vegetables

1. In a bowl, whisk together the egg white, soy sauce and garlic. Add the chicken and toss to coat. Cover and refrigerate for at least 1 hour and up to 1 day.

2. Remove the chicken from the marinade, allowing any excess to drip off. Sprinkle all sides with the sesame seeds and place on a baking sheet brushed with oil. Bake at 190°C, Gas 5, for 5 minutes per side or until the chicken is no longer pink inside.

3. Meanwhile, for the dipping sauce, stir together the jam, water and mustard in a small bowl.

*Make toasted sesame seeds in advance by roasting seeds at 150°C, Gas 2, for 10 minutes. Make extra and store in an airtight jar in the fridge.

EXPRESS ORIENTAL SALMON WITH LEEKS

If the fish is frozen just extend the cooking time by a couple of minutes. This dish is so easy and tastes delicious.

Prep time **5** minutes   Total time **15** minutes

2 salmon fillets, about 125–150g (4–5oz) each
1 leek, thinly sliced (white and light green part only)
1tbsp soy sauce
1tbsp lemon juice
½ tsp ground ginger
Freshly ground pepper
Sides Suggestions (see Basics page 49)
Basmati rice
Wilted greens

1. Prepare the rice as per Basics instructions and prepare the vegetables.

2. In a microwaveable dish mix the soy sauce, lemon juice and ginger. Sprinkle in the leeks and top with the fish, turning once to coat.

3. Cover with clingfilm, leaving a small gap for steam, and microwave on high for about 5 minutes until the fish is opaque and flakes easily with a fork. If your microwave does not rotate, turn the dish after 2½ minutes.

TOMATO AND CHEESE BAKED FISH

An easy weeknight dish.

Prep time **5** minutes   Total time **25** minutes

2x125g (4oz) fish fillets, e.g. halibut, haddock, trout or tilapia
1 medium tomato, chopped
2 spring onions, chopped
1 small clove of garlic, minced
½ a small chilli pepper, de-seeded and finely chopped
1tbsp lemon juice
2tsp grated lemon zest
1tsp olive oil
¼ tsp each salt and pepper
3tbsp reduced-fat grated Cheddar cheese

Sides Suggestions (see Basics page 49)
Wholemeal pasta
Green beans
Tossed salad

1. Prepare the pasta as per Basics instructions and preheat the oven to 220°C, Gas 7.

2. Meanwhile, in a bowl, toss together the tomatoes, onion, garlic, chilli pepper, lemon juice, lemon zest, olive oil, and salt and pepper.

3. Arrange the fish fillets in a small or square baking dish; top with the tomato mixture and sprinkle with the cheese. Bake in the oven for 15–20 minutes or until the fish flakes easily with a fork.

STIR-FRIED SCALLOPS IN BLACK BEAN SAUCE

Prep time **15** minutes   Total time **25** minutes

2tsp vegetable oil
125ml (4fl.oz) chicken or fish stock or water
1tbsp black bean sauce
1tsp cornflour
1 clove of garlic, crushed
1tsp sesame oil
1 celery stick, chopped
½ a red pepper, cored and chopped
90g (3oz) fresh shiitake mushrooms, stems trimmed and sliced
100g (3½ oz) green cabbage, shredded
7 or 8 raw scallops, corals removed, if liked
2 spring onions, sliced on the diagonal
2tbsp chopped fresh coriander, optional

Sides Suggestions (see Basics page 49)
Basmati rice
Salad

1. Prepare the rice as per Basics instructions. In a small bowl, whisk together the stock, cornflour, black bean sauce, garlic and sesame oil.

2. Heat the oil in a wok or large nonstick frying pan over a medium-high heat. Stir-fry the celery, red pepper, mushrooms and cabbage for about 5 minutes, or until the cabbage is tender-crisp.

3. Add the scallops, spring onions and sauce, then stir-fry until the scallops are cooked and the sauce is thickened, about 3 minutes. Garnish with coriander if using.

EXPRESS SALMON PASTA

1tsp rapeseed or vegetable oil
1 small onion, finely chopped
2 cloves of garlic, crushed
500ml (18fl.oz) chicken or fish stock
90g (3oz) wholewheat macaroni pasta
125g (4oz) chopped broccoli or mixed chopped vegetables
90g (3oz) reduced-fat cream cheese with herbs
1x200g can red salmon, drained
Pinch each of salt and freshly ground pepper
1tbsp chopped fresh flat-leaf parsley

Sides Suggestions (see Basics page 49)
Fennel and pear salad with light mayo dressing

1. Prepare salad.

2. Heat 1 teaspoon of the oil in a saucepan over a medium-high heat and cook the onion and garlic for about 3 minutes or until softened. Add the stock and bring to the boil. Add the pasta, cover, reduce the heat to a simmer and cook for 10 minutes. Stir in the broccoli and cream cheese and remove from the heat. Let it stand, covered, for 10 minutes.

3. Flake the salmon lightly with a fork and add to the pasta mixture. Season with pepper and stir gently to combine. Sprinkle with parsley.

Note: You can substitute any of your favourite mixed frozen vegetables for the broccoli.

BRAISED WHITEFISH

Prep time 5 minutes **Total time 25 minutes**

250g (9oz) fillets of halibut, haddock or tilapia
2tsp grainy mustard
2tsp lemon zest
¼ tsp pepper
1tsp olive oil
½ an onion, chopped
4 cloves of garlic, peeled
⅛ tsp salt
Large handful of washed leaf spinach
125ml (4fl.oz) vermouth or dry white wine

Sides Suggestions (see Basics page 49)
New potatoes
Stir-fried lemony vegetables

1. Prepare the potatoes as per Basics instructions. Preheat the oven to 200°C, Gas 6.

2. Rinse and pat the fish dry with a paper towel. In a small bowl, stir together the mustard, lemon zest and pepper. Coat the fish on all sides with the mixture, then set aside.

3. Heat the oil in a large ovenproof frying pan over a medium-high heat. Add the onion and garlic and cook for 5 minutes, or until softened. Reduce the heat to medium and stir in the spinach and salt. Pour in the vermouth or wine. Place the fish on top of the spinach mixture, cover and cook in the oven for 15 minutes or until the fish flakes with a fork.

SAUTÉED HALIBUT WITH TOMATOES AND ANCHOVY

Prep time **5** minutes   Total time **20** minutes

1tbsp olive oil
2 fillets of halibut, about 125g (4oz) each
Pinch of salt
Freshly ground pepper to taste
4 anchovies, chopped
2 cloves of garlic, crushed
¹/₈ tsp cayenne pepper, or to taste
2tbsp chopped parsley
3 plum tomatoes, chopped and seeded

Sides Suggestions (see Basics page 49)
Linguine
Asparagus
Mixed greens salad

1. Prepare the pasta as per Basics instructions.

2. Heat the oil in a nonstick frying pan over a high heat. Season the fish with salt and pepper. Sauté for 1 minute per side, then cover and cook for 5 minutes over a medium-low heat or until the fish is done (see Basics page 49).

3. Remove the fish to a side dish and keep warm. Add the remaining oil to the pan and cook the garlic, cayenne pepper, anchovies and parsley for 3 minutes. Add the tomatoes and cook for another 2 minutes. Serve the sauce over the fish.

CITRUS FISH STEAKS

In South American cuisine, fish is 'cooked' in citrus juices, sitting for at least 6 hours. Here we provide a tangy citrus flavour the express way.

| Prep time **5** minutes | Total time **20** minutes |

(includes 10 minutes marinating)

1 marlin or tuna steak, about 250g (9oz)

For the marinade:
1tbsp olive oil
½ tsp dried thyme
1 clove of garlic, crushed
1tsp lemon juice
1tsp lime juice
¼ tsp freshly ground black pepper

Sides Suggestions (see Basics page 49)
Basmati rice
Green beans or fennel

1. Prepare the rice as per Basics instructions. To make marinade, just whisk together all the ingredients. Place the fish steak in a small dish and pour on the marinade, turn to coat it and let it sit for 10 minutes.

2. Heat the grill or a nonstick pan over a medium-high heat and cook the steak for about 4 minutes per side until medium-rare, or until desired doneness. Cut in two and serve.

COCONUT PRAWN CURRY

Don't be alarmed by the long list – it takes only minutes to assemble.

Prep time **10** minutes   Total time **20** minutes

2tbsp orange juice
1tbsp Thai fish sauce
   (optional)
1tsp cornflour
2tsp soy sauce
1tsp plus 1tbsp vegetable oil
1 small onion, chopped
1 clove of garlic, crushed
½ tsp green curry paste or to
   taste
4tbsp reduced-fat coconut
   milk
8 large prawns, shelled and
   de-veined

1 red pepper, cored and sliced
1tbsp lime juice
1tsp sugar substitute
3tbsp chopped fresh coriander
1tbsp unsalted peanuts,
   chopped

*Sides Suggestions (see Basics
   page 49)*
Basmati rice or spaghetti
Sugar-snap peas
Spinach, rocket and
   watercress salad

1. Prepare the rice or pasta as per Basics instructions.

2. Meanwhile, in a bowl, whisk together the orange juice, fish sauce if using, cornflour and 1 teaspoon of the oil. Stir in the prawns and marinate for 5 minutes.

3. In a large nonstick frying pan, heat 1 tablespoon of oil over a medium-high heat. Cook the onion and garlic for 5 minutes or until softened. Add the curry powder and cook for 1 minute. Add the red peppers and prawns and cook for 2–3 minutes until pink. Stir in the coconut milk, lime juice and sugar substitute and cook for 2 minutes. Garnish with coriander and peanuts.

Note: If you wish to use cooked prawns, add them right at the end for about 30 seconds to warm.

SALMON, RED POTATO AND ASPARAGUS SALAD

Prep time **5–10** minutes Total time **15** minutes

with cooked salmon

180g (6oz) cooked salmon or 1x200g can salmon, drained
2tsp olive oil
¼ tsp salt
¼ tsp pepper
250g (9oz) asparagus, woody ends removed and cut diagonally
    into 1cm (½ in.) pieces
6 new potatoes, cooked and quartered
150g (5oz) cherry tomatoes, cut in half
3 spring onions, chopped
3tbsp chopped fresh mint
150g (5oz) salad greens or baby leaf spinach
For the vinaigrette:
2tbsp extra virgin olive oil
2tbsp lemon juice
½ tsp grated lemon zest (optional)
¼ tsp each salt and freshly ground pepper

1. In a steamer basket placed over a pot of boiling water, cook the asparagus, covered, until just tender, about 5 minutes. Rinse the asparagus under cold water until cool, then set aside.

2. To make the vinaigrette: In a small bowl, whisk together the olive oil, lemon juice, lemon zest if using, salt and pepper.

3. Toss the salad greens with half of the vinaigrette and divide between two plates. Break the salmon into bite-size chunks and place in a large bowl. If you are using canned salmon, drain, place in a bowl and flake lightly with a fork. Add the potatoes, asparagus, tomatoes, green onions, and mint: carefully toss with the remaining dressing. Spoon over the greens.

EXPRESS COCOA SPICE-RUBBED GRILLED STEAK

2tbsp cocoa spice rub (recipe below)
1tbsp olive oil
1 clove of garlic, crushed
250g (9oz) sirloin or rump steak
Sides Suggestions (see Basics page 49)
Green salad
Grilled flat-top mushrooms or other vegetables
New potatoes or rice

1. Cook the potatoes or rice as per Basics instructions.

2. Meanwhile, in a bowl, stir together the rub mix, olive oil and garlic. Rub the mixture into all sides of the steak. Place the steak on a greased grill over a medium-high heat and grill for about 8 minutes, turning once, or until medium-rare inside. Grill the mushrooms, if using, at the same time. Slice the steak thinly and serve on top of a green salad.

COCOA SPICE RUB

2tbsp cocoa
2tsp ground turmeric
1tsp ground cumin
1tsp ground coriander
1tsp ground allspice
1tsp ground cardamom
½ tsp salt
½ tsp pepper

1. In a small bowl, mix all the ingredients together. Keep in a small screw-top jar for up to 6 months.

Makes about 45g (1½ oz)

BEEF AND PASTA

Prep time 5 minutes **Total time 25 minutes**

90g (3oz) wholewheat penne or other pasta shapes
180g (6oz) extra-lean minced beef
1 small onion, chopped
2 cloves of garlic, crushed
½ a courgette, chopped
½ a red pepper, cored and chopped
125g (4oz) mushrooms, chopped
2 medium tomatoes, chopped
4tbsp tomato pasta sauce
2tbsp chopped fresh flat-leaf parsley
2tsp dried basil
¼ tsp salt
½ tsp pepper

Sides Suggestions (see Basics page 49)
Light Caesar salad

1. In a large pot of boiling water, cook the pasta until *al dente*, about 10 minutes, then drain.

2. In a large nonstick frying pan, cook the beef and onion over a medium-high heat until browned, about 8 minutes. Add the garlic, courgette, carrot, red pepper and mushrooms and cook, stirring occasionally, until the vegetables have softened, about 6 minutes.

3. Add the tomatoes, tomato sauce, basil, salt and pepper; simmer for 5 minutes. Stir in the noodles and parsley.

Vegetarian version: Use vegetarian 'minced beef' e.g. Quorn mince or TVP/soya granules – add these after the onion has softened.

CHILLI CON CARNE

Always a favourite, this quick version still has great flavour. You can double this recipe and freeze half for another day.

Prep time **10** minutes   Total time **30** minutes

250g (9oz) extra-lean minced beef
1 onion, chopped
1 red pepper, chopped
1 green bell pepper, chopped
2x400g cans chopped tomatoes
250ml (9fl.oz) water
1tsp chilli powder or to taste
½ tsp ground cumin (optional)
1tsp dried basil
1tsp dried oregano
1x400g can red kidney beans, drained and rinsed
1x200g can sweetcorn, optional
2tbsp reduced-fat crème fraîche or 2tsp reduced-fat grated
    Cheddar cheese

Sides Suggestions (see Basics page 49)
Mixed greens salad

1. In a deep nonstick frying pan cook the onions and beef, stirring until browned, about 8 minutes. Add the peppers, tomatoes, water, chilli powder, basil, oregano and cumin. Cover and simmer for 20 minutes.

2. Add the beans and corn and cook for 2 minutes. Serve with a dollop of reduced fat crème fraîche or grated cheese.

Vegetarian options: Use any minced meat alternative such as Quorn or a half-cup of bulgur instead of beef.

Tip: You can vary the vegetables according to your taste.

VEAL PICCATA

You could use turkey steaks, chicken breasts or pork fillets instead of veal.

Prep time **5** minutes   Total time **25** minutes

250g (9oz) veal medallions
½ tsp salt
¼ tsp freshly ground pepper
2tsp extra virgin olive oil
250g (9oz) mushrooms, sliced
1x400g can artichoke hearts, drained and halved
1tsp dried sage leaves
2tbsp lemon juice
½ tsp lemon zest
2tbsp chopped fresh flat-leaf parsley

Sides Suggestions (see Basics page 49)
New potatoes
Green beans

1. Prepare the potatoes as per Basics instructions. Sprinkle the veal with ¼ tsp of the salt and the pepper.

2. Heat half of the oil in a large nonstick frying pan over a medium-high heat. Cook the veal for 2 minutes per side, or until browned and a slight hint of pink remains. Remove to a plate and keep warm.

3. Return the frying pan to the heat and add the remaining oil. Cook the mushrooms, artichokes, sage and remaining salt for 15 minutes or until the mushrooms are beginning to brown. Add the lemon and simmer for 1 minute. Pour the sauce over the veal and sprinkle with parsley.

PORK TENDERLOIN WITH APPLE AND ROSEMARY

Prep time **5** minutes   Total time **30** minutes

2tsp vegetable oil
250g (9oz) pork tenderloin, cut into 2 pieces
1 small onion, thinly sliced
½ tsp dried rosemary or 1tsp fresh chopped rosemary
4tbsp apple juice
1tsp cider vinegar
1 firm apple, halved and thinly sliced
2tsp currants
¼ tsp curry powder, optional

Sides Suggestions (see Basics page 49)
Basmati rice or new potatoes
Brussels sprouts

1. Prepare the rice or potatoes as per Basics instructions. Heat the oil over a medium-high heat in a nonstick frying pan. Sear the pork on all sides and remove to a side dish.

2. Lower the heat to medium-low and cook the onions, rosemary and curry powder, if using, until the onions soften, about 5 minutes. Add the apple juice and vinegar and cook for 2 minutes. Add the apples and currants and return the pork to the pan. Cover and cook for about 15 minutes until the pork is no longer pink. Slice the pork and serve with apples and onions.

SPEEDY PORK AND LENTILS

Prep time 15 minutes　　**Total time 30 minutes**

90g (3oz) green lentils
350ml (12fl.oz) water
1 small lemon wedge
½ a celeriac, about 200g (7oz), peeled and cut into 1 cm (½ in.)
　chunks
2tsp olive oil
¼ tsp dried thyme
Pinch of salt and freshly ground pepper
1 small onion, chopped
1 small clove of garlic, crushed
6oz pork tenderloin, cut in slices
4tbsp Marsala or red wine
1tsp Dijon mustard

Sides Suggestions (see Basics page 49)
Mixed greens salad
Sliced tomatoes with balsamic vinaigrette

1. Place the lentils, water and lemon in a medium-size pot. Bring to the boil and simmer for 20 minutes or until tender. Drain and place back in the pot, discarding the lemon wedge.

2. Meanwhile, preheat the oven to 220°C, Gas 7. Place the celeriac in a shallow baking dish and toss with 1 teaspoon of olive oil, the thyme, salt and pepper. Bake in the oven for 15 minutes or until just tender. Add to the pot with the lentils.

3. Heat the remaining oil in a nonstick frying pan over a medium-high heat. Cook the onion and garlic for 5 minutes or until softened. Add the pork and cook for 2–3 minutes or until the pork is browned but still pink inside. Stir in the Marsala and Dijon mustard and bring to the boil. Reduce the heat slightly and cook for 2 minutes or until the sauce is thickened slightly. Serve over the lentils and celeriac.

PORK CHOPS WITH PEARS AND GINGER

Prep time **10** minutes | Total time **25** minutes

2 boneless pork loin chops, about 125g (4oz) each,
    trimmed of fat
¼ tsp each salt and freshly ground pepper
1tsp olive oil
1 leek (white and light green parts), halved lengthwise and
    sliced
1 Williams or Comice pear, cored and cut into eighths
2tsp grated fresh ginger
½ tsp sugar substitute
125ml (4fl.oz) chicken stock
1tbsp apple cider vinegar

Sides Suggestions (see Basics page 49)
Rice to soak up the sauce
Sautéed spinach or kale

1. Prepare the rice as per Basics instructions. Meanwhile,
sprinkle the pork chops on both sides with salt and pepper.
Heat the oil in a nonstick frying pan over a medium-high heat.
Add the chops and cook for 3–4 minutes per side or until a
slight hint of pink remains in the centre. Remove to a plate.

2. Add the leeks, pears and ginger to the frying pan. Sprinkle
with the sugar substitute and cook, stirring frequently, until the
leeks are softened and pears are turning golden. Pour in the
chicken stock and apple cider. Allow to simmer for 3–5 minutes
or until the pears are softened and the sauce is reduced slightly.
Return the pork and any accumulated juices to the frying pan.
Simmer for 2 minutes or until the pork is heated through.

Variation: Apples may be substituted for the pears.

BULGUR AND CHICKPEA CHILLI

Prep time **10** minutes   Total time **30** minutes

1tbsp vegetable oil
1 small onion, chopped
2 cloves of garlic, crushed
1 celery stick, chopped
1 carrot, chopped
1tsp chilli powder, or to taste
2tsp dried oregano
½ tsp ground cumin
1x400g can chopped tomatoes
125ml (4fl.oz) vegetable stock
½ x400g can chickpeas, drained and rinsed
50g (1¾ oz) bulgur wheat
1 red pepper, cored and chopped
¼ tsp each salt and pepper

Sides Suggestions (see Basics page 49)
Mixed greens salad

1. Heat the oil in a large pot or nonstick frying pan over a medium heat. Cook the onion, garlic, celery, carrot, chilli powder, oregano and cumin for about 5 minutes or until softened.

2. Add the tomatoes and vegetable stock and bring to the boil. Add the chickpeas, red pepper and bulgur; reduce the heat and simmer for about 20 minutes or until the bulgur is tender. Add salt and pepper and serve.

EXPRESS SAUTÉED GREENS WITH GINGER

Prep time **5** minutes   Total time **15** minutes

2tsp vegetable oil
1 small onion, chopped
4 baby bok choy, chopped coarsely
250g (9oz) curly kale, ends trimmed and chopped
4tbsp vegetable stock or water
2tbsp soy sauce
½ tsp sesame oil, optional
1 clove of garlic, finely chopped
1tbsp finely chopped fresh root ginger
1x400g can chickpeas, or other beans, drained and rinsed
1tbsp sesame seeds, toasted, optional

Sides Suggestions (see Basics page 49)
Top with cooked chicken or turkey breast slices or add 4oz
    cubed tofu with garlic and ginger

1. Heat the oil in a nonstick frying pan or wok over a medium-high heat and cook the onion until soft, about 3 minutes. Add the bok choy and kale, and stir-fry for 2 minutes. Add the stock, soy sauce and sesame oil, if using; bring to the boil. Add the garlic and ginger, reduce the heat to medium, cover and cook for 5 minutes or until the vegetables are tender-crisp.

2. Add the chickpeas and simmer until the beans are thoroughly heated. Sprinkle with the sesame seeds, if using.

CURRIED QUINOA SALAD

You can adjust the amount of curry powder used to give this salad more or less of a kick.

Prep time **20** minutes   Total time **30** minutes

Serves 2 or 3

90g (3oz) quinoa, rinsed and drained

1tbsp plus 2tsp olive oil

2tsp chopped shallots

½–1tsp curry powder, to taste

1tbsp lemon juice

½ tsp Dijon mustard

Pinch each of salt and freshly ground pepper

1 small carrot, finely chopped

¼ of a red pepper, cored and finely chopped

4 dried apricots, chopped

3–4 cashews, chopped

1 spring onion chopped

2tsp chopped fresh parsley

Sides Suggestions (see Basics page 49)

Quorn 'chicken' slices

Broccoli spears

1. In a nonstick frying pan over a medium heat, roast the quinoa for 5 minutes or until fragrant and beginning to pop. In a small saucepan, bring 250ml (9fl.oz) water to the boil. Add the roasted quinoa with a pinch of salt, cover and simmer over a medium heat for 15 minutes or until the water has been absorbed. Scoop the quinoa into a large bowl and cool.

2. Meanwhile, in the same nonstick frying pan, heat 1 tablespoon of oil over a medium-high heat; cook the shallots for 3 minutes or until softened. Stir in the curry powder, to taste, and cook, stirring, for another 2 minutes. Remove from the heat and set aside.

3. In a small bowl, whisk together the remaining olive oil, lemon juice, mustard, salt and pepper and pour it over the quinoa. Stir in the carrot, red pepper, apricots, cashews, green onion and parsley, then serve.

This dish can be covered and refrigerated for up to 3 days.

Non-vegetarian version: *Add a few slices of grilled chicken.*

CREAMY GARLIC FETTUCCINE WITH TOFU AND SPROUTING BROCCOLI

A low-Gi cream sauce! You can use Swiss chard, broccoli or chopped asparagus instead of sprouting broccoli.

Prep time **10** minutes   Total time **25** minutes

125g (4oz) low-fat cottage cheese
2tbsp light cream cheese
1tbsp grated Parmesan cheese
1 small clove of garlic, crushed
⅛ tsp ground nutmeg
⅛ tsp pepper
2tsp olive oil
200g (7oz) firm tofu, cut in small cubes
90g (3oz) wholewheat fettuccine or linguine
125g (4oz) sprouting broccoli, trimmed and chopped

Sides Suggestions (see Basics page 49)
Cos salad with balsamic vinaigrette

1. In a food processor, purée the cottage cheese, cream cheese, Parmesan, garlic, nutmeg and pepper until smooth.

2. Heat the oil in a nonstick frying pan over a medium-high heat. Brown the tofu on all sides for about 2 minutes, then remove to a plate.

3. In a large pot of boiling salted water, cook the fettuccine for 6 minutes. Add the sprouting broccoli and cook for 3–4 minutes or until the fettuccine is *al dente* and the broccoli is just tender. Drain well and return to the pot. Add the tofu and cheese mixture, tossing to coat well with the sauce, then serve.

AUBERGINE PARMESAN

(🕐) Prep time **5** minutes   (🕐) Total time **20–25** minutes

1tbsp grated Parmesan cheese
1tsp Italian herb seasoning
¼ tsp each salt and freshly ground pepper
1 medium aubergine, cut into 1cm (½ in.) slices
1tbsp olive oil
125g (4fl.oz) tomato pasta sauce
2tbsp grated reduced-fat mozzarella cheese
1tbsp chopped fresh flat-leaf parsley or basil, optional

Sides Suggestions (see Basics page 49)
Lean low-fat pork sausages or Peppered Quorn Steaks
Wholewheat noodles
Grilled tomatoes and peas
Mixed salad

1. Prepare the pasta as per Basics instructions. Meanwhile, in a small bowl combine the cheese, Italian herb seasoning, salt and pepper. Brush the aubergine slices with oil and sprinkle the mixture on both sides.

2. Place the aubergine on a greased griddled pan over a medium-high heat and cook for about 15 minutes, turning once, until tender, then remove to a shallow heatproof dish. Heat the pasta sauce gently, pour over the aubergines and sprinkle with the mozzarella and parsley or basil, if using, then serve.

Frying pan option: If a grill is unavailable you can cook the aubergine in a nonstick frying pan or grill pan with 2 teaspoons of olive oil.

QUICK TOFU WITH PENNE AND FETA

Prep time **5** minutes   Total time **15–20** minutes

90g (3oz) wholewheat penne or other pasta shape
2tsp olive oil
200g (7oz) firm herbed tofu cut into 1cm (in.) cubes*
1 small clove of garlic, finely chopped
½ a courgette, chopped
½ a green pepper, cored and chopped
½ tsp dried oregano
½ tsp dried basil
Pinch of salt and freshly ground pepper
2 large tomatoes, seeded and chopped
2tbsp balsamic vinegar
125g (4oz) reduced-fat feta cheese, crumbled

1. Cook the pasta as per Basics instructions. Heat 1 teaspoon of oil in a nonstick frying pan over a medium-high heat and brown the tofu. Add the garlic, courgette, pepper, basil and oregano and cook for 2–3 minutes. Add the tomato and cook for another 2–3 minutes until the tomato softens.

2. Drain the pasta when *al dente* and add to the frying pan. Add the cheese and stir gently, then serve.

If herbed tofu is not available use plain tofu and add extra dried herbs

EXPRESS SALADS

Express salads to use with cooked chicken, lean ham steak or fish
   Use these salads with cooked poultry breast, lean deli meats, fish and seafood, or meat alternatives for a quick dinner. All make great side dishes.

MIXED BEAN SALAD

Prep time **10** minutes   Total time **15** minutes

Serves 2–3

250g (9oz) green beans, trimmed and cut into 2.5cm (1in.)
   pieces
1x400g can mixed salad beans, drained and rinsed
1 red pepper, cored and chopped
½ a small red onion, chopped
2tbsp red wine vinegar
1tbsp extra virgin olive oil
1 clove of garlic, crushed
1tsp Dijon mustard
Pinch each of salt and freshly ground pepper
1tbsp chopped fresh flat-leaf parsley
½ a small cos lettuce, shredded

1. In a saucepan of boiling water, cook the beans for 5 minutes or until just tender. (Alternatively, microwave on high for 3 minutes.) Drain and rinse under cold water until cool. Drain well again and place in a large bowl. Add the canned beans, red peppers and onion to the bowl.

2. In a small bowl, whisk together the vinegar, oil, garlic, mustard, salt and pepper. Pour over the bean mixture with the parsley and toss to coat evenly.

3. Divide the cos between 2 plates. Spoon the bean mixture over the lettuce mixture and serve.

WARM SPINACH AND BACON SALAD WITH CRANBERRY VINAIGRETTE

This bistro-style salad makes a satisfying lunch.

Prep time **10** minutes   Total time **15** minutes

4 slices back bacon
150g (5oz) fresh baby leaf spinach
1 small apple, chopped
4tbsp cranberry juice
2tsp red wine vinegar
1tsp Dijon mustard
¼ tsp sugar substitute
Pinch each of salt and freshly ground pepper
2tsp dried cranberries
1tbsp sunflower seeds, toasted

1. In a nonstick frying pan, cook the bacon over a medium-high heat. Allow to cool, then chop or snip into small pieces.

2. In a large bowl, toss together the spinach and apple.

3. In a small saucepan, whisk together the cranberry juice, vinegar, mustard, sugar substitute, salt and pepper. Add the cranberries and heat the dressing until it is just warmed.

4. Pour the dressing over the salad and toss to coat. Sprinkle with the bacon and sunflower seeds and toss again. Serve immediately.

SUPER EXPRESS: COLD NOODLE SALAD WITH CUCUMBER AND SESAME

This is fancy enough for guests but takes only minutes. Serve with cooked fish or chicken.

Prep time **5** minutes   Total time **10** minutes

90g (3oz) thin pasta or noodles
4tsp rice vinegar
1tsp sugar substitute
2tsp soy sauce
1tbsp sesame seeds, toasted
¼ cucumber, seeded, quartered and sliced
½ a small carrot, grated
1 spring onion, sliced on diagonal

Sides Suggestions (see Basics page 49)
Cooked fish or poultry
Asian vegetable mix

1. Cook the pasta in boiling water until *al dente*. Drain and rinse under cold water, then place in a large bowl.

2. In a small bowl stir together the vinegar, sugar substitute and soy sauce. Pour over the noodles and stir in the remaining ingredients. If you like, this can be served with chunks of cooked fish or sliced chicken breast.

COBB SALAD

This American classic was created in the 1920s and exists in hundreds of variations. Here is a quick version but you can create your own variety using your favourite vegetables.

Prep time **10** minutes   Total time **10** minutes
(15 if cooking bacon)

1 romaine lettuce, torn in bite-size pieces
1 apple, cored and sliced in thin wedges
½ an avocado, sliced
1 tomato, cut into 8 wedges
150g (5oz) cooked chicken or turkey breast, chopped
2 slices of back bacon, cooked and chopped, optional
2tsp grated reduced-fat Cheddar cheese or crumbled blue cheese

Dressing for two:
2tbsp low-fat yogurt or mayonnaise
2tbsp apple juice
1tbsp balsamic vinegar
1½ tsp olive oil
¼ tsp sugar substitute
Pinch of salt and freshly ground pepper

1. Toss the lettuce with the apple and avocado and assemble on two plates. Place the tomato wedges around the sides. Top with the cooked chicken and cooked bacon, if using, and sprinkle with the cheese.

2. Prepare the dressing by mixing all the ingredients in a small jar with a lid. Shake well. Serve on the side and use for dipping. Alternatively, you can toss the dressing with the lettuce salad.

COTTAGE CHEESE SALAD

This creamy crunchy salad can be stuffed into a wholemeal pita, and is also lovely with crispbreads.

Prep time **15** minutes   Total time **15** minutes

1x200g carton low-fat cottage cheese
1 celery stick, chopped
2 radishes, finely chopped
1 spring onion, chopped
1 small apple, cored and chopped
1tsp grated fresh ginger
1tsp soy sauce
1 small clove of garlic, crushed
½ tsp rice wine vinegar
¼ tsp sesame oil

In a bowl, stir together the cottage cheese, carrots, celery, radish, green onions, apple, ginger, soy sauce, garlic, rice vinegar and sesame oil. Then divide between 2 plates and serve.

WARM LEMONY ROASTED VEGETABLE PASTA SALAD

Toss in some leftover roast chicken or a can of tuna or salmon for a simple lunch or dinner. And you can try different vegetable combinations.

Prep time **15** minutes   Total time **30** minutes

1tbsp chopped shallots
1tbsp olive oil
1tbsp lemon juice
1tbsp Dijon mustard
1tbsp chopped fresh herbs (choose from a mixture of thyme, rosemary, oregano, marjoram)
¼ tsp each salt and freshly ground pepper
1 small aubergine, quartered, then cut crosswise into 1cm (½ in.) slices
1 red pepper, cut into 1cm (½ in.) pieces
1 courgette, halved and cut into 1cm (½ in.) rounds
1 small red onion, cut into wedges
125g (4oz) fresh shiitake mushrooms, stems trimmed and caps cut in quarters
90g (3oz) wholewheat penne or other pasta shapes
1tbsp chopped fresh basil or parsley

1. Preheat the oven to 220°C, Gas 7. In a large bowl, whisk together the shallots, oil, lemon juice, mustard, herbs, salt and pepper. Add the vegetables and toss to coat with the dressing. Place in a shallow roasting dish and roast for 20–25 minutes, stirring once, until the vegetables are golden and tender.

2. Meanwhile, in a large pot of boiling salted water, cook the pasta for 8 minutes or until *al dente*. Drain and transfer to a large bowl. Add the cooked vegetables and basil, tossing well. Serve warm or at room temperature.

BROCCOLI AND CAULIFLOWER SALAD

If you double the quantities below, add some cooked chicken, lean ham or turkey breast, you'll have lunch prepared for the next day. You can substitute any fresh herb you want for the tarragon.

Prep time **10** minutes   Total time **30** minutes
including marinade time

250g (9oz) broccoli heads, trimmed into florets
1 small cauliflower, trimmed into florets
½ a red onion, chopped
2tbsp extra virgin olive oil
4tsp lemon juice
1tbsp Dijon mustard
1tsp chopped fresh tarragon
Pinch of salt and freshly ground pepper

1. Steam the broccoli and cauliflower for about 5 minutes or until just tender.

2. In a large bowl, whisk together the olive oil, lemon juice, mustard, tarragon, pepper and salt. Add the broccoli, cauliflower and red onion; toss to coat. Allow to marinate for at least 20 minutes before serving.

Storage: This can be chilled for up to 3 days.

DESSERTS

Plenty of desserts are ideal for the *Express Gi Diet*, as they require no preparation at all, such as:

- fruit yogurt
- berries with yogurt
- cottage cheese with fruit
- medium scoop of no-added-sugar ice cream

If you have a little more time on your hands, or if you have guests coming, you may want to give the following a try, all of which can be prepared in a matter of minutes. We have included here a few recipes suitable for at least four people. Three take only five minutes to prepare and three take a few minutes longer. Enjoy.

MELON AND BERRIES

Prep time **5** minutes   Total time **5** minutes

Serves 4

1 honeydew melon, halved, seeded, peeled and cut into thin slices
400g (14oz) blackberries or raspberries
2tsp lime juice
150g carton natural low-fat vanilla or lemon yogurt, optional

1. Place the melon in a bowl and gently toss with the lime juice.

2. Spread the slices in a fan formation on four plates. Sprinkle with the berries and a dollop of yogurt, if liked.

RASPBERRY FOOL

Prep time **5** minutes   Total time **5** minutes

Serves 4

1x200g carton fat cottage cheese
250g (9oz) frozen raspberries
2tbsp sugar substitute or to taste
1–2tsp amaretto, optional

In a food processor fitted with a steel blade, process the cottage cheese, raspberries, sugar substitute and amaretto, if using. Divide between 4 small dishes or glasses and serve immediately. Alternatively, chill for up to 3 days.

FANCY FRUIT SALAD

Use pretty glass serving dishes and layer the fruit for effect. You can vary the fruit combination for colour and taste.

Prep time **10** minutes   Total time **10** minutes

Serves 4–6

400g (14oz) strawberries – reserve 4 for topping, slice the remainder
400g (14oz) raspberries or blackberries
1tsp sugar substitute, optional
2tbsp orange juice
½ tsp cinnamon
¼ tsp nutmeg
4 kiwi fruits, peeled and sliced
Sprig of mint (optional)

1. Sprinkle the berries with sugar substitute, if using. In a small bowl stir together the orange juice, cinnamon and nutmeg. Layer the fruits in the dishes, ending with slices of kiwi on top.

2. Drizzle each dish with a small amount of the orange juice mixture and top with a whole strawberry. Serve with strained yogurt on side (see page 118).

MICROWAVE CRUMBLE

Cooked in the oven, crumbles require half an hour or more to bake. But in the microwave they take about six minutes.

Prep time **10** minutes   Total time **16** minutes

if using microwave

Serves 6

400g (14oz) fresh or frozen berries, thawed if necessary

2 large dessert apples, cored and chopped

2tbsp wholemeal flour

1tbsp sugar substitute

½ tsp cinnamon

Topping:

150g (5oz) jumbo porridge oats

60g (2oz) pecans or walnuts, chopped

4tbsp sugar substitute

½ tsp vanilla extract

3tbsp non-hydrogenated soft margarine e.g. Biona or Pure, melted

1tsp cinnamon

1. Combine the berries and apple in a 20cm (8in.) microwaveable baking dish. Mix together the flour, 1 tablespoon of sugar substitute and the cinnamon. Sprinkle over the fruit and toss gently to combine.

2. For the topping, mix together the oats, 4 tablespoons of sugar substitute, the vanilla, margarine, pecans and cinnamon. Sprinkle the topping over the fruit mixture and microwave on high for about 6 minutes or until the fruit is tender. Cool for 10 minutes before serving.

Tip: This is delicious served with some low-fat vanilla yogurt.

HOT APPLE SLICES

You can use pears in place of the apples.

Prep time **5** minutes   Total time **15** minutes

Serves 4
2tsp non-hydrogenated margarine, e.g. Biona or Pure
2 Granny Smith or Braeburn apples, cored and sliced
3tbsp sugar substitute
1tsp cinnamon
½ tsp ground ginger
125ml (4fl.oz) apple juice
125 ml (4fl.oz) water

1. Melt the margarine in a nonstick frying pan over a medium-high heat. Add the apples, and sprinkle with the sugar substitute, cinnamon and ginger. Pour in the apple juice and water. Bring to the boil and simmer for 10 minutes or until the apples are softened and the juices are syrupy.

2. Cool and serve with a dollop of low-fat yogurt with sweetener or no-added-sugar ice cream such as Wall's Soft Scoop Light.

ROASTED PEACHES

Prep time **5** minutes   Total time **20** minutes

Serves 4

2 ripe fresh peaches, halved and stoned
1tbsp non-hydrogenated margarine, e.g. Biona or Pure, melted
1tbsp sugar substitute, or to taste
½ tsp vanilla extract
Cottage cheese or quark (skimmed-milk soft cheese), to serve

1. Preheat the oven to 200°C, Gas 6. In a baking dish or ovenproof frying pan, mix the margarine with the vanilla and sugar substitute. Place the peaches, cut-side down, in the baking dish.

2. Bake for about 15 minutes or until the peaches are soft and the skins are starting to wrinkle.

3. Serve the peaches cut-side up, with a spoonful of cottage cheese or quark and juices from the pan.

STRAINED YOGURT

Strained yogurt with a little sweetener or some fruit spread stirred in makes a creamy addition to fresh fruit or a delicious topping for crumbles

Place natural low- or no-fat yogurt in a sieve lined with cheesecloth, a clean household (J) cloth or a coffee filter. Place the sieve over a bowl, cover with clingfilm and chill for at least 1 hour. Discard the liquid that drains off and transfer the yogurt to another bowl. Sweeten with sugar substitute to taste. You can also make flavoured yogurt cheese using any flavoured low-fat yogurt with sweetener.

SNACKS

Snacks are a big part of the Gi Diet and even more so with the Express Gi Diet. We recommend three snacks a day: mid-morning, mid-afternoon and before bed. Many readers have commented that they seem to be eating all the time and are still losing weight!

Busy people frequently find themselves with little time to eat and that's where snacks can really help. All snacks are portable and, with the exception of dairy-based foods, do not require refrigeration. From fruit, vegetables and nuts to delicious muffins, snack bars and scones, there are plenty of choices to keep on hand during your busy day.

With baked goods, such as muffins or snack bars, we recommend you make these in bulk (12–24 at a time) and keep them in the freezer at home. Simply take one out when needed and microwave – or take one into the office where they will naturally defrost before you need them. The time invested upfront will give you a dozen or so ready snacks with no further preparation, and the results will be well worth the effort.

I have grouped the snacks into two categories: ready-to-go snacks that require little or no preparation, and those that have simple recipes that can be made up in bulk every couple of weeks and frozen.

The important thing to remember is to keep your tummy busy digesting food. My 96-year-old old mum likes to say, 'The devil finds work for idle hands.' Well, your tummy works very much along the same principle; if it's not kept busy, it starts looking for its next sugar fix!

READY-TO-GO SNACKS

There are many possible combinations of foods to give you a balanced snack. Here are some of the most popular ones.

- Fruits (fresh or frozen): apples, pears, berries, oranges, etc., with fat-free yogurt and sweetener, or low-fat cottage cheese
- Vegetables: celery, carrots, tomatoes, cucumbers, etc., with hummus, or extra-low-fat cheese e.g. Laughing Cow light/Boursin light
- Low-fat fruit yogurt with sweetener and a few flaked almonds
- Low-fat cottage cheese with a tablespoon of low-sugar fruit jam (where fruit, not sugar, is the first ingredient listed)
- Skimmed milk
- Ice cream: Wall's Soft Scoop light
- Nuts: almonds, peanuts, hazelnuts, soy nuts or macadamia (a small handful)
- Food bars: look for 50–65g bars, around 200 calories, with 20–30g carbohydrates, 12–15g protein and 5g fat per bar, e.g. Slim Fast/Myoplex (½ bar = 1 serving)

RECIPES

Although these snack recipes require some time to prepare, it's well worth it for the convenience of being able to just take one out of the freezer and into the microwave. Try to limit yourself to one muffin or bar a day, though.

You'll see that all measurements for sugar substitute are given in tablespoons rather than by weight. This is because sugar substitute weighs significantly less than granulated sugar and is measured in equal *volume* to sugar, not weight, i.e. one tbsp sugar equals one tbsp substitute.

Muffins

These are unquestionably the most popular snacks, giving lots of variety and being easy to make. Here are a couple of delicious recipes.

MIXED BERRY MUFFINS

Not your average bran muffin. These are moist and packed with berries.

Makes 12 muffins
60g (2oz) All-Bran cereal
50g (1¾ oz) wheat bran
350ml (12fl.oz) buttermilk
2 free-range eggs, beaten
4tbsp vegetable oil
1tsp vanilla extract
125g (4oz) wholemeal flour
8tbsp sugar substitute
1tsp bicarbonate of soda
½ tsp baking powder
350g (12oz) mixture of blueberries and raspberries (fresh or frozen)

1. Preheat the oven to 180°C, Gas 4. In a large bowl, combine the cereal and bran. Stir in the buttermilk, set aside for 5 minutes, then mix in the egg, oil and vanilla.

2. In a separate large bowl, combine the flour, sugar substitute, baking soda and baking powder. Stir into the cereal mixture just until moistened, then stir in the berries.

3. Divide the buttermilk batter among 12 lined or greased muffin cups. Bake in the oven for about 25 minutes or until a thin metal skewer inserted in the centre comes out clean.

Storage: Muffins can be kept at room temperature for about 2 days or, well wrapped and frozen in a resealable plastic bag or airtight container, for up to 1 month.

ORANGE-CRANBERRY BRAN MUFFINS

A popular recipe adapted from the Gi Diet Green Light Cookbook, the cranberries give these moist muffins a nice little burst of tartness.

Makes 12 muffins

25g (1oz) wheat bran
30g (1¼ oz) All-Bran or Bran Flakes
125ml (4fl.oz) boiling water
250ml (9fl.oz) buttermilk
5tbsp sugar substitute
4tbsp vegetable oil
1 omega-3 or free-range egg
1tbsp frozen orange juice concentrate, thawed
1tsp grated orange zest
1tsp vanilla extract

125g (4oz) wholemeal flour
75g (2½ oz) ground flaxseed
1–1½ tsp bicarbonate of soda
1tsp cinnamon
½ tsp ground ginger
¼ tsp salt
225g (8oz) fresh or frozen cranberries, roughly chopped

1. Preheat the oven to 200°C, Gas 6. In a large bowl, combine the bran and cereal. Stir in the boiling water to moisten, then cool for 5 minutes. Mix in the buttermilk, sugar substitute, oil, egg, orange juice, orange zest and vanilla.

2. In a separate large bowl, combine the flour, flaxseed, bicarbonate of soda, cinnamon, ginger and salt; mix in the cranberries. Add to the bran mixture, stirring until just combined.

3. Divide the batter among 12 lined or greased muffin cups. Bake for about 25 minutes or until a thin metal skewer inserted in the centre comes out clean.

Storage: Muffins can be kept at room temperature for about 2 days or, well wrapped and frozen in a resealable plastic bag or airtight container, for up to 1 month.

BARS

Moist and chewy, these bars are a good alternative to fat- and sugar-laden commercial cereal bars. For an extra protein kick, stir in 4 tablespoons of whey or soy-protein powder with the dry ingredients.

BERRY BARS

Makes 16 bars

400g (14oz) raspberries or blueberries, or a mixture of both (fresh or frozen)
150g (5oz) jumbo porridge oats
60g (2oz) high-fibre cereal , e.g. All-Bran or Bran Flakes
50g (1¾ oz) ground flaxseed
3tbsp wheat germ
30g (1¼ oz) wholemeal flour
25g (1oz) sesame seeds
2tsp ground cinnamon
2 egg whites
4tbsp unfiltered apple juice
2tsp vanilla extract

1. Preheat the oven to 180°C, Gas 4. In a large bowl, stir together the berries, oats, cereal, flaxseed, wheat germ, flour, sesame seeds and cinnamon.

2. In a small bowl, whisk together the egg whites, apple juice and vanilla. Add to the dry mixture, stirring to thoroughly moisten.

3. Press into a greased and lined 20cm (8in.) square baking tin. Bake for 35–40 minutes or until lightly golden and firm. Cool, cut into bars in the tin, then turn out.

Storage: Keep refrigerated in an airtight container for up to 5 days or freeze for up to 1 month.

CRAN-APPLE OATMEAL BARS

Makes 24 bars

450g (1lb) jumbo porridge oats
180g (6oz) wholemeal flour
1tsp baking powder
1tsp bicarbonate of soda
2tsp ground cinnamon
¼ tsp salt
12tbsp sugar substitute
3tbsp non-hydrogenated margarine, e.g. Biona or Pure
180g (6oz) apple sauce or unsweetened baby apple purée
1 omega-3 or free-range egg
1 egg white
2tsp vanilla extract
125g (4oz) dried cranberries

1. Preheat the oven to 180°C, Gas 4. In a large bowl, combine the oats, flour, baking powder, bicarbonate of soda, cinnamon and salt.

2. In another bowl, beat together the sugar substitute and margarine until fluffy. Beat in the apple sauce, egg, egg white and vanilla. Add the oat mixture and stir to combine, then stir in the cranberries. Scoop the dough into a greased and lined 32x22cm (13x9in.) baking tin and bake for 20 minutes or until a thin metal skewer inserted in the centre comes out clean. Allow to cool completely, then cut into bars.

Storage: Keep refrigerated in an airtight container for up to 5 days or freeze for up to 1 month.

SUMMARY – FIVE GOLDEN RULES

If you follow these five golden rules along with your green light menu then you will lose weight painlessly, without going hungry or feeling deprived.

Drink a glass of water with each meal
Always drink a glass of water with your lunch and dinner. Drink early on in the meal as this will fill your tummy and help you feel fuller, sooner.

Divide your plate into three
Visualise your plate in three sections: half the plate containing vegetables (at least two different types); one quarter containing protein (meat, fish, poultry, tofu); and one quarter carbohydrates (potato, rice, pasta).

Watch your serving sizes
There are few restrictions on green light foods, especially fruit and vegetables. Nonetheless, moderation is the watchword. For exceptions, see page 14.

Don't rush your meals
It can take half an hour for the brain to realise the stomach is full, so eat slowly to make sure that you don't overeat. Always put down your fork between mouthfuls.

Eat three meals and three snacks per day
Always eat three meals and three snacks daily. Breakfast is particularly important. Keep your tummy busy all day digesting green light foods.

CHAPTER 6: PHASE TWO: HOW YOU WILL EAT FOR THE REST OF YOUR LIFE

Congratulations! You've reached your new weight target. You're probably feeling like a new person since you started your journey a few months ago. But be warned, you are entering a tricky stage as you shift from weight loss to weight maintenance – the phase you will maintain for the rest of your life.

This is the time when, traditionally, most people blow their diets. They have achieved their weight target and fitted into their dream dress, suit or bikini – then they abandon their diet and return to their old eating habits. Surprise, surprise, a few months later they balloon back to where they started, or worse. Sound familiar? I bet most of my readers have experienced this at least once in their lives.

To avoid this yo-yoing, it is important to make only minor shifts in your diet and to remember that fundamental changes have taken place in your body. Firstly, your body has become accustomed to using fewer calories than in its earlier spendthrift days. You have learned to become more energy-efficient (a popular term these days with global warming!), and have a body that needs fewer calories to function.

Secondly, a lighter body requires less calories to function than a heavy one. To use a car analogy, a small car needs less fuel to run than a big one: in the same way, for instance, a 78kg (12 stone) person needs more calories to function than a 68kg (10 ½ stone) person.

Your leaner and more efficient body now requires significantly fewer calories to function than when you began the programme. So in shifting from losing weight to maintaining weight, you need only increase your calorie consumption very slightly. Remember the equation: to maintain your weight, the energy (calories) taken in has to balance the energy expended.

In Phase Two we suggest you make two principal changes.

- Increase your serving sizes of green light foods by 10–20 per cent, especially the ones where we listed a recommended serving size – meat, pasta, rice, bread, etc.
- Add some yellow light foods to your diet. Wine, bananas, 70 per cent cocoa chocolate and sirloin steak are some popular additions.

This will help you make the transition into the final stage of your journey. Again, moderation is the keyword. If you feel yourself sliding and the weight starts to come back, you know what to do. Simply switch back to Phase One and repeat the process. This time, moderate your changes. A little trial and error is inevitable at this stage so don't panic. You'll find the right balance very quickly.

The bottom line is that Phase Two is only marginally different from Phase One. All the fundamentals of the Phase One plan remain unbreakable. Phase Two just provides an opportunity to make small adjustments to portions and add new foods from the yellow light category.

Make the most of this new-found freedom!

CHAPTER 7: TOP FIVE FAQS
(FREQUENTLY ASKED QUESTIONS)

Out of the thousands of e-mails we've received, here are the five most popular questions, along with our response.

Q1. I am currently on a high-protein (typically Atkins) diet and I want to change to the Gi Diet. If I switch, will I put on some of the weight that I've struggled so hard to lose?

A. Many diets, including popular high-protein ones such as Atkins, are diuretics, which is one of the reasons why these diets let you lose weight so quickly in the short term. That is also one of the reasons why people want to change, as they often don't feel well or look good.

   The Gi Diet will rehydrate you, which means you may well put on a pound or two to start with, but that will be quickly lost as your new diet kicks in, providing you with a steady, healthy weight loss.

Q2. Why don't your recipes have a nutritional analysis like other diet books?

A. One of the cornerstones of the Gi Diet is simplicity. Rather than have you worry about nutritional analysis, counting Gi ratings, calories, grams, etc., we decided to do all the analysis for you and colour code the results. Accordingly, green light recipes have a low Gi rating and are also low in calories, sodium and saturated fats.

Q3. I've been losing weight steadily on the Gi Diet but it's suddenly stopped. What should I do?

A. Unfortunately, weight loss never occurs in a straight line. It always goes in fits and starts, descending from one plateau to another. This is true for women in particular, because of hormonal changes in the monthly cycle.

This is why we talk about **average** weekly weight loss in the book. Sometimes you will lose 1–1.5kg (2–3lb) one week and then nothing at all for a couple of weeks. Don't despair if you find yourself stuck on a plateau for a short period – you will soon come off it and continue to lose weight. Remember, it probably took you many years to gain your current weight, so don't be impatient if it takes a few weeks longer than anticipated to lose it.

Q4. I thought sugar substitutes were bad for your health, so why are you recommending them?

A. Sugar substitutes or sweeteners have been approved by all the major government and health agencies worldwide as being perfectly safe for your health. A great deal of disinformation has been spread by the sugar lobby in the United States, particularly on the Internet.

Some people are sensitive to aspartame but there are many other suitable alternatives. Our particular preference is for Splenda (sucralose), which tastes like sugar but without the calories.

Q5. I'm feeling like a cafeteria cook, trying to eat the green light way while looking after the different food needs of my husband and children. Can the whole family follow the Gi Diet whether they have a weight problem or not?

A. The whole family can and should eat the green light way. In fact, we've had so many questions on this issue that we recently wrote and published *The Family Gi Diet*.

The Gi Diet is a healthy and nutritious way to eat for all the family, whether they be reluctant spouses/partners, junk-food-possessed teens or finicky toddlers. By simply making small adjustments to serving sizes, all the family's nutritional needs can be met. Importantly, you will be teaching your children to eat in a healthy way, which will stand them in good stead in the future.

CHAPTER 8: EXERCISE

While exercise is essential for good health and weight maintenance, to be honest it is not that imperative when it comes to losing weight. To illustrate this, have a look at the following table, which shows how much exercise you need in order to lose *just ½ kg (1lb) of fat.*

EFFORT REQUIRED TO LOSE 1LB OF FAT

	9-stone person	11-stone person
Walking (4mph–brisk)	53 miles/85km	42 miles/67km
Running (8min/mile)	36 miles/58km	29 miles/46km
Cycling (12–14mph)	96 miles/154km	79 miles/127km
Sex (moderate effort)	79 times	64 times

Clearly, unless you are an Olympic athlete, this is not the most practical way to get weight off. Don't misunderstand me, any exercise will help to reduce weight, but changing your diet will have a far greater impact on helping you reach your target weight during Phase One. In the long term, if you are to maintain your weight and health, exercise is an essential component. Yet, despite good intentions, there just doesn't seem enough time in the day to devote to getting and keeping your body in shape.

The answer is to incorporate some activity into your daily routine so that it doesn't become that 'added extra' you never seem to have time for. I call this activity the 'Two Stops Short' programme.

TWO STOPS SHORT

As most readers have to travel from home to work, simply get off the bus or underground two stops short of your work destination. At the end of the day, get on two stops further down the road, where you disembarked in the morning. If driving, park between half a mile and one mile before your usual parking spot.

For most people this will represent about 15 minutes brisk walk each way. That's probably no more than 10 minutes' incremental time each way compared to staying on the bus or parking closer. Plus you'll save on fares and maybe be able to park more cheaply!

I did this personally for several years and can vouch for the fact that the results will amaze you. If you do this year round you will use up the energy equivalent of 4½ kg (10lb) of fat. You will also feel healthier, more energetic and sleep better. Not a bad investment in return for just 20 incremental minutes a day!

This method will also afford you some peaceful thinking time in your own company. Why not try it for a couple of weeks? I promise you'll be delighted with the way you'll soon look and feel.

APPENDIX I

COMPLETE GI DIET FOOD GUIDE

RED	YELLOW	GREEN
BEANS		**BEANS**
Broad		Black — Lima
		Black eyed — Mung
		Butter — Pigeon
		Chickpeas — Pinto
		Haricot/Navy — Romano
		Italian — Soy
		Kidney — Split
		Lentils
BEANS (TINNED)		**BEANS (TINNED)**
Baked beans with pork		Baked beans (low-fat)
Refried beans		Mixed salad beans
		Most varieties
		Vegetarian chilli

BEVERAGES

Alcoholic drinks
Coconut milk
Fruit drinks
Milk (whole)
Regular coffee
Regular soft drinks
Rice milk
Sweetened juice

BEVERAGES

Diet soft drinks (caffeinated)
Milk (semi-skimmed)
Red wine
Unsweetened fruit juices:
Apple
Cranberry
Grapefruit
Orange
Pear
Pineapple
Vegetable juice cocktails (e.g. V8)

BEVERAGES

Bottled water
Decaffeinated coffee
(with skimmed milk,
no sugar)
Diet soft drinks (no caffeine)
Herbal teas
Light instant chocolate
Milk (skimmed)
Tea (with skimmed
milk, no sugar)
Soya milk (low-fat, plain)

RED

BREADS

Bagels
Baguette/Croissants
Cereal/Granola bars
Crispbreads
Doughnuts
Hamburger buns
Hot dog buns
Kaiser rolls
Melba toast
Muffins
Pancakes/Waffles
Pizza
Stuffing
Tortillas
White bread

YELLOW

BREADS

Pitta (wholemeal)
Wholegrain breads
Crispbread with fibre

GREEN

BREADS

100% stone-ground
wholemeal*
Homemade muffins
(see p.121-2)
Wholegrain, high-fibre
breads (2½ to 3g of fibre per slice)*
Crispbreads (high-fibre)*

*Limit portions. See p.14

CEREALS

All cold cereals
except those listed
as yellow
or green light
Instant/quick cook porridge oats
Granola
Muesli (commercial)
Millet

CEREAL GRAINS

Almond flour
Couscous
Rice (short-grain, white, instant)
Rice cakes
Croutons
Amaranth
Millet
Polenta
Rice noodles

CEREALS

Shredded Wheat Bran

CEREAL GRAINS

Corn
Corn flour
Spelt
Wholemeal Cous cous

CEREALS

All-Bran
Alpen Crunchy Bran
Bran Buds
Fibre 1
High-Fibre Bran
Oat bran
Porridge oats (traditional large-flake e.g. Jordan's)
100% Bran
Soya Protein Powder
Steel-cut oats

CEREAL GRAINS

Barley
Buckwheat
Bulgur
Gram flour
Kasha (toasted buckwheat)
Quinoa
Rice (basmati, wild, brown, long-grain)
Soya Protein Powder
Wheatgrain
Wheat berries

RED
CONDIMENTS/SEASONINGS

Croutons

Ketchup

Mayonnaise

Tartar sauce

YELLOW
CONDIMENTS/SEASONINGS

Mayonnaise (light)

GREEN
CONDIMENTS/SEASONINGS

Chilli powder

Extracts (Vanilla etc.)

Flavoured vinegars/sauces

Garlic

Herbs/Spices

Horseradish

Hummus

Lemon/lime juice

Mayonnaise (fat-free)

Lemon/lime juice

Mustard

Peppers (all types)

Salsa (low-sugar)

Soy sauce (low-sodium)

Teriyaki sauce

Worcestershire sauce

DAIRY

Cheese
Chocolate milk
Cottage cheese (regular)
Cream
Cream cheese
Goats' milk
Milk (whole)
Sour cream
Yogurt (regular)
Almond milk
Rice milk
Yogurt (low-fat)
Evaporated milk

DAIRY

Cheese (low-fat)
Cream cheese (light)
Ice cream (low-fat)
Milk (semi-skimmed)
Frozen yogurt
(low-fat, low-sugar)
Soft margarine
(non-hydrogenated)
Sour cream (light)
Sour cream (fat-free)
Crème fraîche (low-fat)

DAIRY

Almond milk (low fat)
Buttermilk (skimmed low fat)
Cheese (fat-free)
Cottage cheese
(low-fat or fat-free)
Fruit yogurt
(fat-free/with sweetener)
Ice cream
(low-fat and no added sugar
e.g. Wall's Soft Scoop Light)
Milk (skimmed)
Laughing Cow cheese/light
Boursin cheese/light
Soy cheese/low-fat
Soya milk (plain, low-fat)
Soy/whey protein powder

RED

FATS/OILS/DRESSINGS

Butter
Coconut oil
Hard margarine
Lard
Mayonnaise
Palm oil
Peanut butter
(regular and light)
Salad dressings (regular)
Tropical oils
Vegetable shortening

*Limit portions. See p14

YELLOW

FATS/OILS/DRESSINGS

Corn oil
Mayonnaise (light)
Most nuts
Peanut oil
100% Peanut butter*
Salad dressings (light)
Sesame oil
Soft margarine
(non-hydrogenated)
Soy oil
Sunflower oil
Vegetable oils

GREEN

FATS/OILS/DRESSINGS

Rapeseed oil*
Flax seed oil*
Mayonnaise (low-fat/low sugar)
Olive oil*
Salad dressings (low-fat/low sugar)
Soft margarine (non-
hydrogenated, light)*
Vegetable oil sprays
Vinaigrette

FRUITS – FRESH

Cantaloupe
Dates
Honeydew melon
Kumquats
Watermelon

FRUITS – FRESH

Apricots (fresh)
Bananas
Figs
Kiwi
Mangoes
Papaya
Persimmon
Pineapple
Pomegranate

FRUITS – FRESH

Apples
Avocado (¼ per serving)
Blackberries
Blueberries
Cherries
Grapefruit
Grapes
Guavas
Lemons
Limes
Oranges
Nectarines
Peaches
Pears
Plums
Raspberries
Strawberries
Rhubarb

RED

FRUITS – BOTTLED, TINNED, FROZEN, DRIED

All tinned fruit in syrup

Apple purée containing sugar

Most dried fruit*

*For bulking, it's OK to use a modest amount of dried fruit.

FRUIT SPREADS

Regular fruit spreads

FRUIT JUICES

Fruit drinks

Sweetened juices

Prune

Watermelon

YELLOW

FRUITS – BOTTLED, TINNED, FROZEN, DRIED

Dried apricots

Dried cranberries

Fruit cocktail in juice

Peaches/pears in syrup

Prunes

FRUIT SPREADS

FRUIT JUICES

Apple (unsweetened)

Cranberry (unsweetened)

Grapefruit (unsweetened)

Orange (unsweetened)

Pear (unsweetened)

Pineapple (unsweetened)

GREEN

FRUITS – BOTTLED, TINNED, FROZEN, DRIED

Apple sauce (no sugar)

e.g. Clearspring Organic

Apple Purée

Dried apples

Frozen berries

Mandarin oranges

Peaches in juice or water

Pears in juice or water

FRUIT SPREADS

Extra fruit/low-sugar spreads

Fruit as first ingredient

FRUIT JUICES

Eat the fruit rather than

drink the juice

MEAT, POULTRY, FISH, EGGS AND SOY

Minced beef (more than 10% fat)
Hamburgers
Hot dogs
Processed meats
Regular bacon
Sausages
Whole regular eggs
Fish/shellfish (breaded/battered)
Sushi (it's the rice)
Pâté
Boiled ham
Offal

MEAT, POULTRY, FISH, EGGS AND SOY

Flank steak
Minced beef (lean)
Sirloin tip
Sirloin steak
Lamb (Tenderloin, Centre loin chop, Boiled ham)
Pork (Fore shank, Leg shank, Centre cut, Loin chop)
Turkey bacon
Whole omega-3 eggs (e.g. Columbus)
Chicken/turkey leg
Fish tinned in oil

MEAT, POULTRY, FISH, EGGS AND SOY

All seafood, fresh, frozen or tinned
Back bacon
Beef (Top round steak, Eye round steak)
Chicken breast (skinless)
Egg whites
Lean deli ham
Minced beef (extra lean)
Pork tenderloin
Quorn
Sashimi
Smoked salmon/trout
Soy/whey protein powder
Tofu
Turkey breast (skinless)
Veal (Cutlet, Rib Roast, Blade steak)
Rabbit
Venison

GREEN

PASTA*

Capellini

Cellophane noodles
(mung bean)

Fettuccine

Linguine

Macaroni

Penne

Rigatoni

Spaghetti

Vermicelli

PASTA SAUCES

Light sauces with
or without vegetables
(no added sugar)

YELLOW

PASTA*

Rice noodles

PASTA SAUCES

Sauces with vegetables

RED

PASTA*

All tinned pastas

Gnocchi

Macaroni and cheese

Noodles (tinned)

Pasta filled with
cheese or meat

Preferably wholemeal or protein-enriched pasta

PASTA SAUCES

Alfredo

Sauces with added
meat or cheese

Sauces with added
sugar or sucrose

SNACKS

- Bagels
- Bread
- Chocolates and sweets
- Coconuts
- Cookies
- Biscuits
- Doughnuts
- French fries
- Ice cream
- Jelly (all varieties)
- Muffins (commercial)
- Peanut butter (regular)
- Popcorn (regular)
- Crisps/Pretzels
- Raisins
- Rice cakes
- Sorbet
- Tortilla chips
- Mixed dried fruit and nuts
- Jellies (all types)

SNACKS

- Bananas
- Dark chocolate (70% cocoa)*
- Ice cream (low-fat)
- Most nuts*
- Peanut butter (100% peanuts)
- Popcorn (light, microwaveable)

*Limit portions. See p.14

**Caution: high sodium

SNACKS

- Almonds*
- Apple purée (unsweetened)
- Tinned peaches/pears in juice or water
- Canned fruits
- Cottage cheese (1% or fat-free)
- Food bars (12–15g protein; 4–5g fat) e.g. Myoplex/Slim Fast*
- Nuts (see fats and oils)*
- Fruit yogurt (fat-free/ with sweetener)
- Ice cream (low-fat and no added sugar e.g. Wall's Soft Scoop Light)
- Hazelnuts*
- Homemade muffins see p121-2
- Marmite**
- Most fresh fruit
- Most fresh vegetables
- Most seeds
- Soy nuts*
- Vegemite**

RED

SOUPS

All cream-based soups
Tinned black bean
Tinned green pea
Puréed vegetable
Tinned split pea

SUGAR AND SWEETENERS

Corn syrup
Glucose
Honey
Molasses
Sugar (all types)
Treacle

YELLOW

SOUPS

Tinned chicken noodle
Tinned lentil
Tinned tomato

SUGAR AND SWEETENERS

Fructose
Sugar alcohols

GREEN

SOUPS

All homemade soups
made with green-light
ingredients
Chunky bean and
vegetable soups (e.g.
Baxter's Healthy Choice)

SUGAR AND SWEETENERS

Aspartame
Hermesetas Gold
Splenda
Stevia

TINNED/BOTTLED VEGETABLES

Roasted red peppers
Tinned tomatoes
Tomato puree

VEGETABLES

Broad beans
French fries
Hash browns
Parsnips
Potatoes (instant)
Potatoes (mashed or baked)
Swede
Turnip

VEGETABLES

Artichokes
Beets
Corn
Potatoes (boiled)
Pumpkin
Squash
Sweet potatoes
Yams

VEGETABLES

Alfalfa sprouts
Asparagus
Aubergine
Beans (green/runner)
Bok choy
Broccoli
Brussels sprouts
Cabbage
Capers
Carrots
Cauliflower
Celery
Collard greens
Courgettes
Cucumber
Fennel
Kale
Leeks
Lettuce
Mangetout
Mushrooms
Mustard greens
Okra
Olives*
Onions
Parsley
Peas
Peppers
Peppers (chillies)
Pickles
Potatoes (new/small)
Radicchio
Radishes
Sauerkraut
Scallions
Sugar snap peas
Swiss chard
Spinach
Tomatoes

APPENDIX 2: SEVEN-DAY MEAL PLAN

Let the sample menu below be a guide, and substitute other recipes and suggestions from this book to suit your taste. Each dinner recipe in the book is accompanied with quick side-dish suggestions to enable you to get dinner on the table in thirty minutes maximum. Enjoy.

MONDAY

BREAKFAST
Porridge (page 58)

SNACK
Fruit yogurt and almonds

LUNCH
Open-faced lean sliced ham sandwich with grainy mustard and salad

SNACK
Orange-Cranberry Bran muffin[1] (page 122)

DINNER
Express Oriental Salmon with Leeks (page 85)

SNACK
Fresh berries tossed in lime juice and low-fat crème fraîche

TUESDAY

BREAKFAST
Muesli (page 57)

SNACK
Carrots, cucumber, sliced peppers, with Laughing Cow light cheese

LUNCH
Salad (page 64)

SNACK
Apple and almonds

DINNER
Chicken Tarragon with Mushrooms (page 76)

SNACK
Canned or fresh peaches with low-fat cottage cheese

WEDNESDAY

BREAKFAST
Porridge (page 58)

SNACK
Berry bars (page 123)

LUNCH
Open-faced tuna salad sandwich[2]

SNACK
2 mini light Babybel cheeses and a pear

DINNER
Speedy Pork with Lentils (page 99)

SNACK
Fruit salad (page 115) with 2 medium scoops low-fat, low-sugar ice cream (e.g. Wall's Soft Scoop Light)

THURSDAY

BREAKFAST
Bran-Delicious Cereal (page 57)

SNACK
Light cottage cheese with fruit

LUNCH
Egg and Veg (page 66)3

SNACK
Mixed Berry Muffins (page 121)

DINNER
Citrus Fish Steaks (page 91)

SNACK
Sliced pears with soya pudding (e.g. Alpro)

FRIDAY

BREAKFAST
Porridge (page 58)

SNACK
Light cottage cheese with fruit

LUNCH
Open-faced lean, thinly sliced chicken or turkey breast sandwich with grainy mustard and salad

SNACK
Orange-Cranberry Bran muffin (page 122)

DINNER
Sauteed greens with ginger (page 102)

SNACK
Fruit yogurt and fresh berries

SATURDAY

BREAKFAST
Smoked Salmon Scrambled Eggs (page 61)

SNACK
Cran-Apple Oatmeal Bars (page 124)

LUNCH
Cobb Salad (page 110)

SNACK
Fruit and almonds

DINNER
Express Cocoa Spice-Rubbed Grilled Steak (page 94)

SNACK
Microwave Crumble (page 116)

SUNDAY

BREAKFAST
Muesli (page 57)

SNACK
Carrots, cucumber, sliced peppers, with hummus

LUNCH
Warm spinach and bacon salad (page 108)

SNACK
Berry bar and fruit

DINNER
Roasted Chicken with Tomatoes and Asparagus (page 78)

SNACK
Raspberry Fool (page 114)

1. Make muffins and muesli bars in bulk on weekends. Wrap individually and freeze.

2. See the section on lunch (page 66) for guidance on sandwich contents and suggestions.

3. Why not give yourself a day off and buy lunch using the recommended lunch suggestions on page 66.

APPENDIX III
GI DIET WEEKLY WEIGHT/WAIST LOG

WEEK	DATE	WEIGHT	WAIST	COMMENTS

WEEK	DATE	WEIGHT	WAIST	COMMENTS

If you had said to me six months ago that by Christmas I would be down to a weight similar to that of my late teens, I would never have believed you! I purchased the first book in June and I, and many people I know, are astounded with the weight loss I have achieved. I have gone from just over 13 stone to 10 stone in 6 months! But the best thing is that I have not had to compromise my love of food. *Susie*

I went to the doctor and was diagnosed with Poly-Cystic Ovarian Syndrome (PCOS). My husband and I were trying to conceive without success. My doctor basically told me if I wanted to have a baby, I would need to lose weight. When I stumbled upon your Gi Diet, I thought it was a Godsend – as if it was specifically designed for me in my time of need! After about 5–6 months, I had lost over 2 stone, which were definitely staying off. Not only was I looking great, but I was feeling great... I am 3 months pregnant expecting our first child in August! Not only did I get pregnant, I got pregnant naturally – without fertility or blood-sugar-related drugs! It's literally a miracle. I thank God for your Gi Diet, though I consider it more of a lifestyle than a diet. It has truly changed my life for the better! Thank you! *Erin*

My daughters bought me your book and I decided to try it, but with little thought that it would work. Anyway, just over a year later I've lost nearly 4 stone and I can walk into any shop I like and buy whatever clothes I like. I feel like a new woman! It's incredible – I've not had so much fun since university days! I love that I can eat so well, but look so good. Everyone is amazed and so many people have bought your books on my recommendation. I have 5 kids and we all eat the same things – they are probably so much healthier now too. So a great big heartfelt thank you. The Gi eating plan is excellent because it works and it's healthy and it's so easy. Keep up the good work. *Roberta*

I am 35 and have been overweight for the past 7 years. My eldest daughter has just turned 5 and is becoming aware of body image issues, and I was extremely worried that all she got from me was 'I hate my fat belly'. I wanted to take the focus away from weight issues and put it onto health issues instead. Now it is, 'We do this to be healthy', instead of 'We do this so we don't get fat'. Well for the past 12 weeks I have been following your Gi diet and I have gone from 10 stone to 8 stone 11 pounds and from size 12–14 to a size 10. Other than the physical benefits, I have been overwhelmed with the psychological impact this has had on me. I now believe I deserve to look good and now invest in good clothing, skincare and hair care. It is quite liberating. Cheers, *Brenna*

INDEX